THE EMPATHIC
GHOST HUNTER

THE
EMPATHIC
GHOST HUNTER

REDFeather

MIND | BODY | SPIRIT

An Imprint of Schiffer Publishing

Bety Comerford and Steve Wilson

Designed by Danielle D. Farmer
Cover design by Justin Watkinson

Type set in Universe LT Std

ISBN: 978-0-7643-5409-0
Printed in China

Published by Red Feather Mind Body Spirit
An Imprint of Schiffer Publishing, Ltd.
4880 Lower Valley Road
Atglen, PA 19310
Phone: (610) 593-1777; Fax: (610) 593-2002
E-mail: Info@schifferbooks.com
Web: www.schifferbooks.com

For our complete selection of fine books on this and related subjects, please visit our website at www.schifferbooks.com. You may also write for a free catalog.

Schiffer Publishing's titles are available at special discounts for bulk purchases for sales promotions or premiums. Special editions, including personalized covers, corporate imprints, and excerpts, can be created in large quantities for special needs. For more information, contact the publisher.

We are always looking for people to write books on new and related subjects. If you have an idea for a book, please contact us at proposals@schifferbooks.com.

You can be a victim
of your life
or you can be a student
of your life.
The choice is up to you.

THE RELUCTANT EMPATH
ISBN: 978-0-7643-4603-3

THE EMPATH'S QUEST: FINDING YOUR DESTINY
ISBN: 978-0-7643-5223-2

GHOST AND SHAMANIC TALES OF TRUE HAUNTINGS
ISBN: 978-0-7643-4128-1

BETY

TO NANCI AND MICHELLE
who never back down from an energetic adventure.

STEVE

TO ALL THE GIFTED MEDIUMS AND PSYCHICS
who helped me navigate the unseen world from this side of the veil and from the next.
You know who you are.

To all friends, family, and enemies who helped me navigate the
emotions of forgiveness.

CONTENTS

INTRODUCTION

Imagine standing in a line in the grocery store and suddenly feeling an overwhelming sadness. You have no clue where it's coming from. You weren't sad two seconds ago. Yet a sorrow so deep starts to bubble up in your chest. You look around. It's then that you notice the woman standing in line in front of you has her head bent. Her mascara is smudged. She's trying to wipe away tears without calling attention to herself.

And so it begins.

Such is the experience of an empath. Some will discount it. Some will run away, trying to avoid such encounters. Others will use all manner of tools and belief systems to try and render themselves immune from the energy of others.

Then there are the ones who will begin the deepest of quests that begins with the question, "why?"

We know it's not polite to stare at or pry in another's personal emotional plight unless we're invited to do so. Many simply back off. As an empath, however, we are still energetically connected in some way to experience this sometimes debilitating and oftentimes draining encounter.

Is it possible that we are designed to experience each other's emotional and physical pain? Are we victims to this? If so, there is that question again—why? Or is it possible that we are asked to experience these moments in order to learn? To gain a greater understanding and knowledge of energy projected from others due to choices they've made? Some of the energy we feel is physical. Some is emotional, mental, and yes, even spiritual. All of this energy we feel has the potential to overwhelm, to create a swamp of heaviness. It's sucked up by every unsuspecting empath who is just trying to survive a harsh world.

But what if that's not exactly true? What if there is more to why you feel all that you feel? What if this energy you're feeling is here to teach you? What if this is in part an answer to human existence? Energy drives all our actions. Empaths know this best. Why? Because you feel it.

But what about the darting shadows? The random feelings? The smells? The quick flashes you suddenly see out of the corner of your eye? Strange dreams and yes, even the sudden appearance of an apparition? How do we gauge their meaning? How do they fit into our energetic world with our limited knowledge of the Other Side?

Many times these otherworldly experiences will drive an empath further into the mindset of hating the fact that they're empaths. They just want all this to go away. They just want to try and live what they think of as a normal life. For some, however, the quest of understanding their empathic gift begins. Why? Because they have no choice. Because they are feeling what they are feeling, no matter what. They are driven to understand it. There's a reason for it. It's not random.

Ask any paranormal investigator what started their delving into the world of ghost hunting and they will probably tell you they too experienced some kind of otherworldly event that, no matter how hard they tried, could not fit into the parameters of what is considered normal.

We have been investigating paranormal situations for more than fifteen years with our group, The Spirit Light Network. As empaths, we have been inundated with the unseen since childhood. We've seen firsthand the interaction between the living and dead. It's much more prevalent than people realize. Rather than prove or disprove the existence of ghosts, we instead took another approach. We wanted to find out *why* the haunting was taking place. What was keeping a ghost stuck in the first place? What was it that made a room feel uncomfortable? Why did battlefields still reverberate with the fear and horror of something that happened centuries before?

We quickly realized, it's all just energy. But within that energy are clues about life. And about the afterlife.

Experiencing the energies of the afterlife gives us a glimpse into the complexity of what they thought, who they were, and the emotional state they were in when they died. These energies cannot be faked. They cannot be mimicked. They are instead a catalogue of a living life brought into the afterlife. It is a testament to the truth of how the spirit lived their life and the choices they made in that life.

Therefore, this book is a little different from your typical how-to book on ghost hunting. It's designed to give you, the empath, and anyone sensitive to energy, some tools and understandings and, hopefully, a comfortability, that you're not crazy when you hear things that go bump in the night. We hope to help you see that you have the potential to be a gift in that energetic moment to the dead. Because of your heightened sensitivities, you have the ability to transmute the heavy emotions that keep a spirit stuck. As we have pointed out in our other books, the greatest ability an empath has is the capability to change the energy around them. You can change, not only the energy of the living, but you can change the energy of the dead as well.

By doing that, you become the gift that allows them to move on. To no longer remain bound to the earth plane. You lighten up a space, a house, a life.

We ask that you keep an open mind as you read the following pages. Know that what you read will be teaching you that the energy we are in our life is important because that is the energy we will take with us when it's our time to pass on. The energy of life follows us into the afterlife. Here begins the responsibility of being in your life to its fullest extent energetically to increase your energetic vibration to what some call light, some call love. By doing that, is it not then possible to light the way for those who wander? For those who seek the light and love they never knew in life?

As we said earlier, we're finding there is much more interaction with the Other Side than people want to admit. So many experiences are happening to empaths that they cannot explain, be it phantom illnesses, phantom pain, phantom emotions, as well as the inexplicable pull to visit certain places, houses, countries.

Hopefully this book can begin to unravel some of these mysteries.

We touched on ghosts in our first book, *Ghost and Shamanic Tales of True Hauntings* and the phenomena of being an empath in our second book, *The Reluctant Empath*. We intend to go deeper here; to explain why the empath feels what they feel from the Other Side and what they can do to work with this particular gift. There seems to be more and more ghost programs on television that have piqued the interest of the public. Unfortunately, they never tell the full story, particularly relating to why a spirit exists and what to do if you're seeing or feeling ghosts. This topic is especially important for parents. Children are much more sensitive than ever before. We are constantly being called upon to assist families where their children are interacting with ghosts. In these pages, we will demystify the phenomena and bring light to a subject that is fraught with fear and misunderstanding.

We have been successful in presenting complex theories through the use of Alex, a stand-in for whoever picks up this book. Within the following pages, Alex will be joined in his empathic adventures by Zoey, Cora, Keri, Nell, and Ariel, students of energy just like Alex. Together, they will use their empathic skills to take you on a journey through the world of the paranormal.

As with each of our books, every story presented here is true, though in some instances we have had to change the names to respect the privacy of the individuals involved. The investigations are ones we actually conducted. The feelings and emotions and realizations were ones we personally experienced. Growing up as empaths, we had no choice but to learn the ways of energy in order to navigate our lives and stay sane from the bombardment of everyone's emotions. Add to that the emotions of the dead and you can see how imperative it was for us to learn what we did. It's now part of our path to present our findings to you so you too can learn to navigate your life through the increasing ups and downs of the world we see, and the world we don't see.

Energy cannot be destroyed. But you can learn to steer yourself through the energetic hurdles that life and death presents to all of us. You can then take your place in this world with a knowing that you don't need to be a victim to this energy. You can retain your sense of self and be the example to others who are still struggling, be it with the energy of the living, or the energy of the dead. Because you see . . .

It's all just energy.

WE'RE NOT ALONE

The deep reds and oranges of the Arizona sunset

The deep reds and oranges of the Arizona sunset enthralled Alex as he sat on a hill overlooking the hotel where he and his companions were staying. Months ago, he'd suddenly had a knowing that he needed to fly to Arizona. He wasn't sure why at the time, but as a spiritual teacher, he'd learned to listen to these feelings. The three women he was with, students from his spiritual classes, also had that same knowing; they too knew they had to go to Arizona. It was a feeling so strong, none could ignore it.

The reasons for their trip soon became apparent. They were on an energetic journey—a set of lessons they each needed to experience to take them to the next level of energetic understanding: of comprehending why they were here in the first place, of why they'd had to live through events in their lives—some painful, some awe inspiring—that brought them to this point in their respective spiritual paths. So far it had been fantastic and unexpected and sometimes beyond words.

As Alex watched the whorls of light in the sky begin to darken, he absently wondered what was next. What was the next lesson or the next energetic experience for him and his friends to encounter? There was an excitement within him that he couldn't deny. His crazy life as an empath, experiencing deep ups and downs and feeling intense joy and crippling depression, was finally making sense. Through the lessons presented to him, he'd learned that the empathic abilities he'd tried to hide from for so long were now a gift to be eagerly embraced.

They still had two days to go before they flew home. What was next on their energetic agenda? He'd no sooner thought of the question than he was confronted with the answer.

While looking out at the sunset, Alex suddenly felt the hairs on the back of his neck stand up. He had the unmistakable feeling that he wasn't alone on the hillside. That wasn't unusual. The hill was next to his hotel and the ground was covered with footprints of people who had climbed this hill before him. Believing a hotel guest had climbed up to see the spectacular view, he turned and looked behind him. To his dismay, there was no one there. Trying to convince himself it was his imagination, he started to turn back when he saw, out of the corner of his eye, a shadow duck behind a pair of boulders that were on the other side of the hill from where he sat.

"Hello? Is someone there?" he called out.

His only response was a light breeze that blew up from the surrounding desert as the skies grew darker.

Before it got too gloomy, Alex stood up and looked behind the boulders. No one was there. Yet the feeling that he was not alone did not lessen. In fact, it began to intensify.

He recalled growing up seeing these darting silhouettes, usually when he least expected it. For lack of a better name, he called them the "shadow people."

There was a difference, however, in how he experienced the shadow people in his youth and how he was experiencing them now. In the past, he'd always reacted with fear. He saw these shadow people as an intrusion, and he wanted them to go away. But now, standing on this hill with the night sky beginning to twinkle with stars, he felt no fear. On the contrary. The sight of the shadow person got his attention. After everything he'd gone through in his life energetically, the fear was now replaced with a curiosity. He wanted to understand what the phenomenon of shadow people was all about. Were they the shadows of people who had died? Were they something darker?

Surrounded by darkness, he should have been unnerved, but to his surprise, he wasn't. Instead, he had a sense that this was the next energetic lesson to learn. These shadow people were going to give him and his companions a different experience with their empathic abilities. What that experience was, he didn't quite know yet. But, as he'd learned over the years, whatever it was would be memorable.

The next morning when he awoke, Alex knew where they had to go. With his heightened awareness of energy, the entire trip so far has been based on where he and companions felt a pull to go. That morning was no different. When Cora,

Keri, and Zoey joined him at breakfast, they saw him sitting with a road map opened in front of him.

"So where are we off to today?" Cora asked as she slid in next to Alex.

Cora had been studying spirituality and energy with Alex for almost a year now. She still had a tendency to impose her strong willpower on everyone, but was growing aware of it and trying her best to curb the habit. She was learning to be okay with where people were on their spiritual path and not judge them.

"We're off to Bisbee. Specifically to the Copper Queen Hotel."

"I've heard of that place," Zoey remarked. Zoey too had studied with Alex for many years. She'd shared many of the same experiences he had, and they'd developed a deep and warm friendship.

"I'm game," Keri replied.

Keri was Alex's newest student, yet she'd come far in a short period of time in understanding and accepting her empathic gifts.

"The name of the hotel was on my mind when I woke up," Alex continued.

Zoey turned the map around and studied it. "You do know that's over six hours away?"

"Then the sooner we get on the road, the faster we'll get there."

"And just what is there?"

Alex smiled, a mischievous gleam in his eye. "You'll see."

Zoey raised an eyebrow. "You know I hate when you do that."

"I know."

The ride was uneventful, and by late afternoon, they were standing in the lobby of the Copper Queen Hotel.

The hotel was finished in 1902 to serve the booming copper mining community that had grown up in Bisbee, Arizona. It still retained an air of the Victorian old West era with its furnishings and large saloon on the first floor.

The group was impressed with what they saw when they finally arrived: A cream-colored building with red trim and a long green painted terrace that snaked along part of the second floor — it looked warm and accommodating.

The foursome stood at the registration desk. Alex immediately noticed a cabinet on the wall behind the counter with several rows of room keys dangling from hooks. It drew his attention as Zoey went about getting accommodations for them for the night.

"We'll need four rooms, preferably near each other," she said.

"That won't be a problem." As the woman at the front desk prepared the paperwork to register them, Alex suddenly felt a shift in energy. It was as though the air about him was growing heavier.

This is interesting, he thought to himself. To his amazement, he saw one of the keys on the cabinet jiggle. He blinked, doubtful of what he was seeing. He turned away, then looked back. Just as he was convincing himself he'd been mistaken, the key jiggled again.

"I'll take Room 315!" he spoke up without thinking.

The woman turned and eyed him for a long moment. "You sure about that?" she asked.

"Positive."

She hesitated, then shrugged. "If that's what you want," she muttered.

After getting registered, they retrieved their luggage and made their way to the third floor. Zoey's room was next door to Alex, while Keri and Cora were down the hall.

All the way down the corridor towards his room, Alex felt a weirdness to the energy. It was as though there was a chilly thickness to the air. Thinking he was just tired from the long drive, he noticed the others were tired as well.

"If it's all the same to you, I think I'm going to hit the sack," Cora said. "For some reason, I'm suddenly exhausted."

"Me too," Keri concurred. "I'll see you guys in the morning."

After Keri and Cora entered their rooms, Zoey was left alone in the hallway with Alex.

"What was that all about downstairs?" she asked. "I thought you were going to jump over the counter and grab the key to this room."

Alex shook his head. "Would you believe me if I told you I actually saw the key jiggle, not once but twice? It's as if I was meant to stay in this room."

Zoey chuckled. "Nothing that happens to you surprises me." She started to turn away, then abruptly turned back. "I didn't want to say anything in front of Cora and Keri, but did you feel that creepy energy downstairs? It was as if we were being watched, but there was no one in the lobby. And up here it feels cold. Not air-conditioning cold. But a cold, like inside my body. Should be an interesting night."

"I agree."

After wishing each other a good night, Alex retired to his room. It was a comfortable room, with a queen-sized bed and old-fashioned wallpaper that helped retain the aura of the Old West. He washed up in the bathroom and was in the process of preparing for bed when once again he felt the air in the room growing thicker. And colder. He knew he was having an empathic energetic experience—as if the vibration in the room spoke of a person being present, only the person was someone he couldn't see.

He felt a chill run down his back. The vibration he felt was not the same as when a spiritual guide appeared. When guidance appeared, the energy felt wonderful. His body would tingle and his vibration would rise; it was as if he was being bathed in white light. This vibration, however, was lower. It was filled with the energy of someone or something that was lurking. Furtive. Hiding.

Alex immediately recognized the vibration.

I'm not alone in this room.

In the past, he would have run away, his own anxiety pushing him out the door. Yet for some reason, he wasn't afraid. He wasn't shunning the experience.

He was actually curious. This opened him up more.

"Who are you?" he asked aloud. "What do you want?"

He felt the energy begin to coalesce. As if he was about to be shown what it was he was feeling. He turned towards the darkest corner of his room and unconsciously held his breath. He could barely discern a white mist begin to take shape. Despite not being afraid, his pulse increased and his eyes widened with amazement. Just a little bit more and he'd see—

BANG! BANG!

His heart nearly gave out when the obscenely loud banging almost broke down his door. Opening it quickly, Cora and Keri stumbled in followed by Zoey. The two women were in hysterics. As their energy filled the room, the thickness in the air abruptly disappeared.

"What's going on?" Alex asked as Cora and Keri, blankets thrown over their pajamas, huddled together on the edge of his bed.

"What kind of place did you bring us to?" Cora cried out.

"If you think I'm spending one more minute in this hotel, you're crazy!" Keri exclaimed.

Alex and Zoey exchanged perplexed looks.

"They banged on my door and insisted I come with them to your room," Zoey explained.

"Calm down," Alex replied. "You're okay now."

"I won't be okay until I'm out of here!" Keri insisted.

It took Alex and Zoey a few minutes to finally calm down their companions.

"I was in bed when I distinctly felt someone bend down over me and whisper my name in my ear," Cora said.

"And I was in the bathroom brushing my teeth when someone actually pulled my hair!" Keri added. "Doesn't this place frighten you?"

Alex shook his head. "Actually, it intrigues me."

"Are you nuts?" Keri exploded. "This place is haunted!"

"I know it is." He then shared his experience seeing the key jiggle behind the front desk. "I believe the work we've been doing in understanding our empathic ability is going to give us some tools that we can use to figure out what's going on here. It's obvious we were meant to check into the Copper Queen tonight. If you two can control your fear, I say we just sit here and see what happens. Can you do that?"

Both Cora and Keri gulped. "I—don't know," Cora admitted.

Alex sat down next to her. "Zoey and I will be right here. Nothing bad will happen. Think about this trip so far. We've been able to get out of our heads and our own emotions and go into the energy of whatever place we find ourselves in. That's allowed us to be open to whatever is going to happen. By doing that, we've had some amazing experiences, haven't we?"

"That's true."

"Then let's trust this too is going to be amazing."

Cora hesitated, then took a deep breath. "Okay. But if something touches me or pulls my hair, I'm out of here."

"If it helps, before you came in here, I was sensing someone in this room. There was nothing evil or violent about them, so there really is nothing to be frightened of. Whatever happens, just stay open."

Cora and Keri nodded. Zoey made herself comfortable in a nearby chair while Alex remained seated next to Cora. The four friends grew quiet. Soon, the only sound they heard was their own breathing. Five minutes passed. Just as Alex was beginning to fear that Cora and Keri would grow restless, he felt the air start to change. His feelings were confirmed when Cora unconsciously clamped her fingers around Alex's hand. To her credit, however, she remained open.

The air grew still . . . then eerily quiet, as if time itself was slowing down. A chill began to be felt as if someone were turning down the thermostat. All sound from outside the hotel ceased to be heard as the air began to be heavy and thick. Something was getting ready to happen. They could all feel it.

"Oh God, oh God, oh God," Cora mumbled in fear as she stared into the corner of the bedroom. The others followed her train of vision and each gasped.

Standing before them was what appeared to be a tall shadow and a short shadow standing next to each other. None of the group could quite believe what they were seeing; Cora actually pinched herself, but the shadows remained.

"What is this sadness I'm feeling?" Keri whispered as her eyes pricked with unexpected tears. "I'm going to cry, and I don't know why."

"I'm not sure, but I'm feeling it, too," Alex concurred.

"I don't know about you, but I'm ready to get the heck out of this hotel," Cora said as she turned and started towards the door. "There is no way I'm staying here with shadows popping up."

Zoey looked at Alex. "I think we should leave too. We're never going to get any sleep here. Besides, it's too creepy."

Alex agreed and the group, after gathering their things quickly, turned their backs on the shadow figures and checked out of the hotel.

STAYING
OPEN

There are so many times empaths, when they have an experience with the living, go into a place of shutting down because it feels uncomfortable. They believe they are powerless in controlling what they're feeling and try their best to retreat from it. This is true even more so with the things that can't be seen. One of the lessons empaths learn quicker than anybody is that many times there is some kind of leftover experience from life into death. How do they know this? Because they feel it. If an empath can remain open to the process of experiencing the emotions of whatever the moment presents, as we know, they can learn energetic information about how life works. And how the choices made in one's life are possibly carried to the other side. This may also explain many of the other physical, mental, and emotional experiences an empath has, especially the ones who seem to have no frame of reference, such as the sudden headache. Could that be the energy of someone who died with head trauma? The tight feeling in the chest— could that be the energy left over from a heart attack or the diseased lungs of a smoker? Add to that a flash of memory from nowhere, or even the smell of tobacco in an empty space where no one is smoking. This begins to point to the knowledge of the energy of life that follows into death. Still, it's only energy. But to an empath who is open, it's part of a grand puzzle piece that, as long as they remain open and curious, will eventually fall into place and make sense.

THE BIRD CAGE

They drove down the road and found a quiet roadside inn. It wasn't as nice as the hotel they'd left, but it was clean. And, more importantly, it was of a newer construction. As many people believe, old spaces usually means old ghosts. They hoped that the new building would mean they wouldn't have to deal with any unseen visitors lurking about.

Still, although unspoken, each wondered if they'd be able to sleep; the memory of the shadows they'd experienced at the Copper Queen were still too vivid. But exhaustion overcame them and they drifted off to sleep.

When Alex got up the next morning, he thought to the night before. Just what had that been all about? He'd seen what he called shadow people before, but last night's experience had been way over the top. Try as he might, he couldn't fully understand what had happened and, the key question he kept coming back to was why had it happened to them?

Knowing he'd just go round and round and get nowhere, Alex pushed the event out of his mind. He met Keri and Cora in the dining room. A few moments later, Zoey arrived. As usual, her curiosity aroused by the events of the night before, she'd gotten up early to use the hotel's Internet. She couldn't wait to share what she'd found. They ordered breakfast and as soon as the waitress walked away, she launched into her findings.

"Well Alex, it seems there was a reason you were drawn to Room 315 last night. I did some research and I discovered that room is supposedly haunted by the spirit of Julia Lowell."

"I never heard of her," Alex admitted.

"The Copper Queen Hotel was always considered a high-class establishment. However, in the 1920s–30s, Miss Lowell served as a female companion who 'serviced' men in Room 315."

"Are you kidding me?" Cora exclaimed.

Zoey shrugged. "Prostitution was tolerated in Arizona at that time, and apparently, Miss Julia Lowell was quite the enchantress. Unfortunately, she fell deeply in love with a man who didn't share her sentiments. She was okay to sleep with, but not to marry. In despair, she killed herself. It's said that she likes to appear to men. Sometimes she'll whisper in their ears. Sometimes they'll awaken to find her doing a seductive strip tease at the foot of their bed."

Alex raised an eyebrow at Cora and Keri. "Look what you made me miss by barging into my room last night," he joked.

"There's also the ghost of a little boy who likes to hide articles from guests who stay on the third floor."

"Then I'm glad we got the heck out of there," Cora replied emphatically. "I don't like the idea of ghosts anywhere near me." Keri nodded in agreement.

Zoey and Alex exchanged glances. If the next step in their spiritual development was learning about ghosts, were Cora and Keri ready for that?

Deciding to let the subject drop, Zoey took a small guidebook from her bag and flipped through the pages.

"How do you guys feel about going to the OK Corral? According to the guidebook, it's about ten minutes down the road."

"Isn't that where Wyatt Earp had his famous shoot-out?" Keri asked.

Zoey nodded. "According to what I read, the Clantons were part of a gang of cattle rustlers, thieves, and murderers. The Earp brothers were brought into Tombstone to help keep the law. The two groups kept having run-ins as each tried to control the growing town of Tombstone. Finally, on October 26, 1881, it climaxed in a thirty-second gun battle at the OK Corral that has gone down in history as the most famous gun battle of the American Old West."

"As long as we don't run into more shadow thingies, I'm game," Keri replied, half jokingly.

An hour later they were standing in front of a small Corral. Surrounding them were re-enactors, dressed in clothing the group recognized from old movies depicting the gun battle. The actors representing the Earps were dressed in long, black duster coats that reached down to their calves. The men playing the Clantons were dressed in light brown pants, boots, and vests. They all wore the essential cowboy hats and also sported six shooters and rifles. Speaking in lazy drawls added to the authenticity of the area.

"It's a lot smaller than I thought," Cora replied.

Standing there, Alex and Zoey started feeling an energy that felt somewhat familiar to them, but that they couldn't explain. It felt as though a heaviness had descended upon their shoulders. They looked about them at the other tourists and at Cora and Keri, but no one seemed to notice the increasingly oppressive energy.

Alex bent low over Zoey and whispered, "This tourist attraction is becoming more than just a tourist attraction. We're in the middle of an energetic experience here that seems to be setting us apart from everyone around us."

"You're right," she responded. In an effort to try and dissipate the energy, Zoey wandered over to a spot to the right of the Corral. Suddenly, she yelped out in pain as she furiously shook her right hand.

"What happened?" Keri asked.

"I don't know. I just suddenly got this pain in my wrist." She moved away from the spot and shook her hand a few times. "Huh. That's strange. The pain is gone."

Alex wanted to say something, but he was finding it difficult to stay present in the moment. While Zoey struggled to understand what had just happened to her, he found himself feeling as though he was there, but not there—almost in a place between realities. Fighting through the disconcerting feelings, he came up beside Zoey and said quietly, "The energy here is weird."

"It's beyond weird. I just felt this sharp pain in my wrist that instantly disappeared when I walked away from the spot where I initially felt it. I'm also having a hard time getting into this place. I love all this historical stuff; I love seeing the women in the dresses and petticoats and the men dressed like cowboys, but I feel like I'm swimming between states of reality, if that makes any sense. It's like I'm here but not here."

He gave her an astonished look. "That's exactly what I'm feeling."

The two glanced over to Cora and Keri. They seemed unaffected by the energy Alex and Zoey were experiencing. They were flirting and taking pictures with the actors portraying Doc Holliday and Wyatt Earp.

"I think they're feeling a whole different type of energy than we are," Zoey joked.

"Let's walk about a bit and see if we can figure out what's going on."

The two strolled down the main street of Tombstone, trying to take in the sights of the numerous old buildings that dotted each side of the main thoroughfare. However, try as they might, each still felt a bit woozy, as though they were stepping in and out of time.

"Do you think what we're feeling is maybe a past-life remembrance?" Zoey asked. "I mean, I've never been here before, but yet I feel like I have."

"I honestly don't know," Alex admitted.

Zoey sighed. "Who knows? Maybe what we're remembering are all the old Westerns on the late show that took place at the OK Corral. My favorite version is still the one with Kurt Russell as Wyatt Earp."

"Nah. Henry Fonda's *My Darling Clementine* is still the best. You can't beat John Ford's direction."

"We can argue the merits of both movies over lunch. I'm starving!"

Seeing that Cora and Keri were still flirting with the reenactors, they took themselves over to an ice cream and sandwich shop where they ordered lunch. They sat outside and ate as they watched the crowds of tourists and guides mill about. When they were done eating, Alex realized he felt better.

"Whatever was going on energetically grounded out when I ate. In fact, I feel restored. Let's explore Tombstone some more."

Zoey shook her head. "You go on. For some reason, I'm suddenly feeling very tired. I don't know if it's a combination of last night and the energy here today, but I just don't feel right. I'm going to sit in the van and chill." She stood up. "One thing I've learned from my empathy is that when enough is enough, I have to trust that. I'll let Cora and Keri know."

"Okay. I'll call you when I'm ready to leave." Alex looked out over the old Western town. "I feel like there's something here I have to figure out."

"Good luck."

As Zoey turned towards the parking lot, Alex strolled down the street. The sun was beating down on him, and he was starting to sweat profusely. He stopped in front of a tan building with the words Bird Cage Theatre painted in large letters on the front. For reasons he couldn't explain, he felt he had to enter. Having learned to trust his instincts, he opened the door and stepped inside.

The air that greeted him was cool and musty, and it felt refreshing after the heat of the Arizona sun.

To his surprise, he was alone. He'd thought the building would be packed with tourists, but as he wandered about, he saw there was no one there. Stepping further within, he found himself in what must have been the original bar. There was a mirror on the wall behind the bar, and mannequins were set up to represent the bartender and one of the saloon girls. The sight of them unsettled Alex. There was something eerily disconcerting about them. Turning away, he climbed the stairs to what turned out to be the theater. The lights were low, and all along the balcony were what appeared to be tiny rooms with curtains. He remembered reading that this is where the "soiled doves," as the prostitutes were called, would entertain their clients during a show. They were called birdcages, giving the name to the theater.

As Alex took in the old, slightly decrepit building, he noticed how the energy seemed to be all over the place. He felt he was being spun around in a washing machine. He shook his head to clear it, wondering why he'd been drawn here.

Moving toward the stage, his attention was riveted to a set of bullet holes in the wall. A sign explained they were indeed bullet holes left by a drunken cowboy who shot at an actor.

"Boy, theater critics were tough in those days," Alex mused to himself. As he bent down to more closely inspect the bullet holes, he saw a shadow dart by. Straightening up, he saw another. From the birdcages, he heard the unmistakable sounds of female giggling. Swerving his head from side to side, he next saw the image of a woman's petticoat run by.

If he was any other kind of man, he would have fled the scene in terror. Instead, his curiosity kicked in. Once again, this oddity in energy intrigued him. Walking slowly along the theater, he noticed the images started to slow and he heard feminine voices surrounding him. To his astonishment, the energy felt almost joyful, as if the unseen females were happy to see him. Or did they know he was even there? Was it possible he'd just walked into an energetic party from the past?

He was about to step out of the theater when, to his surprise, he saw the quick image of a short man, dressed in a sombrero and Mexican clothing before disappearing in the blink of an eye. In that moment, Alex felt an overwhelming sense of machismo energy. He knew the energy wasn't coming from him; it had to be coming from the Mexican he'd just seen.

He stopped and wiped his brow.

This was getting to be a bit too much, even for him.

He'd felt energy before, but never with the stark visualizations that today were accompanying the energies.

With the energy jumping to and fro again, he found himself growing dizzy with the intensity of everything. It was time to leave. As he started towards the front door, he noticed a bookstore/souvenir shop to his right. He walked in and saw a young woman standing behind the register. With long, shiny black hair and dimples in her cheeks, she greeted him with a large, friendly smile. He smiled back and turned his attention to the bookshelf. One of the books immediately caught his eye. On the cover was an old tintype photograph of women in petticoats. To his surprise, he recognized one of the women in the photo as one of the women he'd just seen in the theater.

He picked up the book knowing he had to read it.

Walking up to the register, the girl nodded towards the book in his hand. "That's a great book. You'll enjoy it," she said. She started to say something more, but stopped. Instead, she gently peered at him. "Say, are you okay? You don't look so good."

Without thinking, Alex blurted out, "I don't know how to say this, but what just happened to me upstairs has me a little shell shocked."

"You mean in the theater? What happened?"

"I think I saw the women on this cover running around up there."

The girl audibly gasped. "You've *seen* them?"

"Yeah. And who is the Mexican running around up there as well?"

She gasped again. "You've seen him, too? Oh my God! I thought I was the only one who saw them. We've had a couple of ghost hunting groups come through, but they don't see what I've seen. You're the first person who says they've seen the ghosts here. Especially the Mexican. No one ever sees him. I was starting to think I was certifiably nuts."

Giving into the energy of curiosity, Alex looked at her. "Do you want to go back upstairs with me?"

The young woman studied him. Alex could sense she was feeling his own sense of curiosity and wondered if she too was an empath. He hoped she'd say yes; by returning to the theater together, it would serve to validate both their experiences.

"Sure," she finally nodded. "My boss isn't here and it's almost closing time. I'll show you some places that are closed off to the public."

They went back upstairs and together their curiosity and the combined energies of the two of them seemed to magnify the energy in the theater. The ghostly images of the prostitutes were now visibly running by, their giggles filling the musty air. The Mexican occasionally showed himself, trying to menace Alex before disappearing again. The two were enthralled by all they were experiencing; both seeming to interact, but at the same time, feeling the hodgepodge of energy and emotion all around them.

"Thank you," Alex said once they'd returned downstairs.

"No, thank *you*! I thought I was going crazy, but now I know I'm not."

Stepping back out into the hot sun, Alex called Zoey and told her what had happened. After gathering the others, they all met back at the van.

"You look like you've seen a ghost," Keri said as she looked at Alex's face.

"You have no idea."

At dinner that night, Alex shared with the group what he had experienced at the Bird Cage Theatre. "I don't know what's happening, but for some reason things that I've seen and experienced throughout my life—these shadow people—are appearing to me more and more. It's actually getting to be too much. Yet I know there's something we need to learn from this."

"You know, when I was young, I was always talking about my friends that no one else could see," Zoey replied. "My parents thought I was nuts and encouraged me to stop talking about them. Finally I did, and they gradually disappeared."

"I hear that a lot," Alex said. "But why is this happening? People are coming in and out of my space as if doors have opened and they're stepping in. For some reason, I think these shadow people can now see us. It's creating some sort of connection between us and them, as if a light switch has been turned on and they're actually trying to get our attention."

"But why do they want to get our attention? And just what are these shadows anyway?" Keri asked.

"All I know is that when I first arrived in Tombstone, I felt out of sorts. It was a struggle to get my bearings on what I was feeling as an empath. Whatever this energy today was, however, I couldn't settle down. Eating lunch helped me center myself. As I wandered about, my curiosity made my intuition stronger, and it seemed as though the shadows were actually manifesting as someone I could equate as male or female. The weird part is that I don't know what I was feeling from them. It wasn't fear, but I just don't know. As to what they are, they seem to be ghosts. Maybe they're in shadow form because they don't have enough energy to fully manifest yet, or maybe we just haven't evolved enough to a point where we can fully see them."

Zoey said, "You know we talk a lot about these phantom feelings that seem to come out of nowhere. Like last night when we all felt sad. Today, when I went back to the van, I started reading about the gun battle at the OK Corral. And guess what? Billy Clanton was shot in the wrist by Morgan Earp. Is it possible we're feeling something from either the shadow people or ghosts that are still hanging around? Who's to say Billy Clanton isn't still stuck at the spot where he died such a violent death? Maybe my empathy somehow linked me to him in such a way that I actually felt his pain when he got shot in the wrist."

Alex thought about it for a moment. "That's a good point." He paused, then continued, "Well, there's only one way to figure this all out. We obviously need more experience. This whole trip has been about experiencing. As empaths, we constantly find ourselves stuffed into places to experience and to learn from those experiences. Therefore, when we get home, we really need to pay attention. Somehow I get the feeling the answers we're looking for will be back where we started."

CHANGING YOUR PERCEPTION

So many times in our lives, we find ourselves reacting fearfully to things we don't fully understand. As empaths, we know from experience this reaction releases a frequency of energy that is of a very low vibration. Most wouldn't call fear a fun experience. Add to that all the other reactions based in fear, and it doesn't take long to see what an energetic swamp has been created. Due to our experiences navigating the angers, feelings, and emotions of the living, what if we, as empaths, begin to decipher these situations differently? What if we learn to see this as an opportunity to change how we react in any given moment? If we approach energy in another way, is it possible to bring the situation to a higher vibration or a space of excitement because we know we're about to learn something? As we've discovered, when we don't plug into situations, our own vibration increases. Add to that the energies of other like-minded empaths. Instead of a jumble of fear, anger, and that sickly syrupy feeling most empaths feel, a window begins to open. Could it be this is why empathic people seem to have more paranormal experiences?

The vacation sadly came to its inevitable conclusion. They'd each learned so much on this trip. It was as though time had been suspended so they could experience all they had. But now it was time to return to "reality."

On the plane ride home, Zoey sat quietly looking out the window at the passing white fluffy clouds, musing on the trip. It had been extraordinary on so many levels. Yet the core foundation of all they'd been through was to try and comprehend what they were feeling at any given moment and understanding why they were feeling what they were feeling. She'd come to understand that the situations they'd encountered weren't haphazard or random. Each had been presented as an opportunity to learn something new about their empathic abilities. This latest lesson about shadow people and ghosts was a case in point. They'd just finished learning the lessons regarding the timeline—a map of each individual's life which holds all their lessons (from *The Empath's Quest: Finding Your Destiny*). As an empath, surrendering to the timeline allowed one to be propelled forward towards their destiny. Now they were ready to move on to the next set of lessons presented to them on their timeline.

Every person on the planet had the same opportunity to learn whatever lessons were on their timeline. Some chose to learn, others did not. Zoey knew she and Alex weren't special. What did, however, set them apart was an intense desire to understand why they felt what they did. They wanted to know where they fit into the world and what their empathic abilities meant. They especially wanted to learn how to navigate their lives on a planet that seemed to be sinking deeper and deeper into fear and violence with both of them feeling all that negativity and heaviness at every turn.

One of the most important lessons Zoey had learned from Alex over the years was not to become a victim to what she was feeling at any given moment. Instead, she was compelled to understand the mechanics of the energy she was experiencing. She shared this innate curiosity with Alex and it was this curiosity that cancelled out the fear factor. Rather than have a knee-jerk reaction and try to block everything out, as she knew many empaths did, she strove to comprehend it. That was partly why she and Alex had risen above being victims to their empathy.

As she liked to tell Alex, before they'd met, she'd reached a point in her life where she'd become sick and tired of being sick and tired. She knew there had to be a better way to live with her empathy. Meeting Alex and taking part in his spiritual classes, he'd shown her that indeed, there was a better way. It hadn't always been easy. But it was never boring.

As if reading her mind, Alex turned to her and said, "We need to explore this ghost thing further. We need to figure out what this energy and the shadow people are all about. I've seen shadow people all my life, but yesterday was way over the top, even for me. I believe this is happening as part of learning what it means to be empathic."

Zoey smiled. "Are you basically telling me we need to have more interaction with ghosts?"

Alex chuckled. "I guess I am."

Zoey thought about it for a moment. "Well, there are public ghost hunts, especially at Halloween that I always see advertised. That's only a month and a half away. I'll keep an eye out and see if something jumps out that we simply have to go to."

"Sounds like a plan." She grinned at him, then turned her attention back out the window while Alex settled down with the book he'd bought at the Bird Cage Theatre.

The clouds outside the plane disappeared as Zoey cast her mind back over the years since she'd first met Alex.

Twenty years had passed since their fateful encounter at the home of a mutual friend. They'd hit it off immediately, and as they got to know each other, she'd begun to feel towards him the same emotions as she would a cherished brother. They had an understanding, a connection that transcended the labels people put on such a close relationship between a man and a woman. There was no need for physical attraction; rather it was an attraction of their minds and their energy, which created a push to comprehend their lives and where they fit in. They knew they could tell each other anything, and there would be no judgment. They saw themselves in the bigger picture—two souls on an incredible journey who, no matter what, always had each other's backs.

Zoey knew how lucky she was to find a friend like Alex. As she struggled to understand the spiritual concepts he presented, he was always patient, no matter how badly she herself thought she'd failed. Determined to get it right, she was grateful for his counsel.

One of the things that impressed her most about Alex was his ability to remain calm in any given situation. They'd had some amazing adventures trying to understand their empathy, but no matter how things got "way over the top," he never succumbed to fear, or anger, or anxiety. In the midst of a hurricane, he always stayed true to his center and didn't plug in. He remained in a calm state, able to look at the experience from different angles.

He also, no matter what, refrained from getting caught up in others' drama. Zoey inwardly cringed when she recalled how she would so easily find herself swept up in her friends' or family's drama. She'd come to see over the years how many people *thrived* on drama. If there wasn't any, they created it. It was how they received energy. By eliciting reactions in others, they gathered the energies of those reactions to themselves.

Alex was the first person she'd ever met who was, for lack of a better description, anti-drama. And that was the secret to why he was able to take on whatever lessons the Universe threw at him. Without losing his composure to whatever drama was playing out around him, he would instead slowly and painstakingly keep at it until he understood whatever it was the energy was trying to teach him. Zoey was sure when he was young, he'd probably freaked out when things happened that seemed out of the ordinary. It was natural. But over the years, he'd evolved into a man who made others feel safe in his presence—who took a situation and dissected it until he came to a conclusion that made sense.

Zoey understood why. When an empath is bombarded with emotions, they always feel worse when they react. And as she knew from personal experience, an empath quickly becomes drained when they "leak" their energy by reacting. However, by remaining calm, it's easier to navigate and understand why something is happening.

Zoey inwardly smiled when she realized that for years, she'd been a reactor. She'd had no road maps growing up as an empath. In fact, there were times she thought she was going crazy because she felt smothered by all she was feeling. She would lash out, or sink into depression, or simply withdraw from the world.

I also spent years expecting people to be a certain way. Of course they never were and I always ended up disappointed and hurt, she thought.

Alex taught her that, as she had the freedom to choose to learn from the lessons presented to her, so did everyone else. It took a great deal of courage to accept the challenges these lessons provided. Not everyone had that courage. According to Alex, that was okay. As a spiritual person, all she could do was meet people wherever they were on their own journey.

Alex had also shown her that as she healed her issues, it helped her see the bigger picture—not only for herself, but for those around her. She saw where they were on their own timeline. Her own energy, lightening up as she healed, offered the example to others that just as she went through the sometimes painful process of healing, so could they. Her energy, no longer burdened by the weight of her own emotional baggage, also gave permission to others to begin their own exploration of why they were created and what their purpose was. By not judging and having no expectations of others, her energy became the energy of truth. That truth allowed others to drop their masks and discover who they really were.

All of this manifested because Alex chose not to be a victim of his life, because he chose to be curious rather than reactionary. He in turn, shared this with others, serving as the example that it could be done. These others, which included Zoey, then paid it forward by serving as examples to others.

Maybe this is how we change this crazy world — by changing one person at a time, beginning with ourselves, she thought.

It was a heady thought, but just as Alex had changed Zoey's world, she and his other students had the potential to change others' worlds. All it took was courage and curiosity. Of knowing there had to be a rhyme and reason to their lives—they just had to find it.

It wasn't easy. There were many times Zoey watched Alex be taken advantage of because of his warm, non-judgmental nature. Still, he stuck to his conviction that everyone has the opportunity to rise to the occasion—to react in a different way than how they've always reacted. To realize there's more to life than getting one up on someone, of amassing the most "toys," or having to feel superior. If they didn't rise to the occasion, so be it. They'd have another opportunity and another. And if they never changed, well, there was always the next life to get it right.

It wasn't that Alex was a rainbows and unicorns kind of guy. On the contrary. But he exemplified his spiritual beliefs. And to her, that was something to admire and emulate.

And now they were about to embark on the lessons surrounding the interaction between the living and the dead.

Zoey turned to Alex and tugged at his sleeve. "Tell me, what are you hoping to learn in this next set of lessons?"

He thought for a moment, then began counting out on his fingers, "Number one, what exactly are shadow people? If they're spirits, why do they only appear in shadow? Number two, why did our energy feel out of sorts when we went to the OK Corral yesterday? Number three, why did we feel what can only be described as phantom pain when we stood where the shooting took place? Number four, why did our energy increase when that girl from the gift shop and I stood together in the Bird Cage Theater?" He took a breath and looked at her. "I've been thinking about it and the conclusion I've reached is that somehow, someway, the energies we feel from the living are the same as those we feel from the dead. It's the only explanation that makes sense."

"And you want to prove that theory by having more interaction with the dead?" Zoey asked.

"I think that's the only way to do it."

Zoey paused for a long moment, then gave a nod. "I think you're right. But if any of those spirits take a shine to me and follow me home, I'm going to personally strangle you."

Alex laughed. "Then let's hope the next set of lessons provides a way to deal with that."

YOU'RE NOT A
VICTIM

So many people who call themselves empaths find themselves living a life of overwhelming emotion, a prison from which they cannot escape. Many search for answers in the medical world, others in religious traditions. Some fall prey to substance and/ or food abuse. Some all of the above. The harsh reality is that many times isolation becomes the relationship of choice. It's easier to be by one's self than to feel the lower energies of the world around them. But what if being an empath doesn't include believing yourself a victim? Instead, being an empath gives you a wonderful opportunity to learn the skills and abilities energy presents.

Autumn was Alex's favorite time of year. He loved the changing colors of the leaves, the cool briskness of the fall nights. While people grumbled about the early darkening of the days, he instead found a calmness in the dark evenings. As he'd learned over the years, as long as you carried the light within your heart, you could go into the darkest of places and always stay illuminated.

Following up on their experiences in Arizona, Zoey got into the habit of dropping off at Alex's apartment on Friday nights, laden with a pizza or Chinese take-out to watch the latest television programs on ghost hunting. They hoped these shows would provide some of the answers they were seeking in their quest to understand ghosts and the reasons they haunted. Keri and Cora were asked to participate, but both bowed out, admitting they had absolutely no interest in having any contact with the dead.

"What happened in Alex's hotel room in Arizona is enough to last me a lifetime," Cora replied emphatically.

As it was, the only good thing about those Friday nights was the food. As they watched show after show, they realized the energy they were feeling from these programs didn't feel good. Something felt off.

Finally after a few weeks, Zoey sat back on Alex's sofa with a thud. "I don't get it. All these shows are the same. It's a bunch of men and women running around with instruments trying to prove the existence of ghosts. Then, if they do prove there's a ghost, they basically wave good-bye at the end of the program and leave. They don't do anything about the spirits or offer an explanation why they're stuck. Nor do they try to un-stick the spirits, so to speak. I don't know how to feel about this. Should I feel sorry for the owners, the hunters, or the ghosts?"

"They obviously don't know how to un-stick the ghosts," replied Alex.

Zoey smiled. "I don't know why I'm complaining. We don't either."

Alex took a bite of his tuna sushi roll. "I hear what you're saying, though. I'm not quite sure why, but these shows are leaving me feeling crummy rather than enlightened. The teams are either full of bravado or full of fear and all are full of judgment regarding the spirits. And, despite saying they're experts in the field of ghost investigations, some of them scare the people who are being haunted half to death with nonsensical advice. None of them seem to be able to just stay open minded in the moment and allow whatever is supposed to happen to unfold."

"They have ratings to worry about. They don't have time to just stand there and wait."

He looked at her, his eyes twinkling. "Guess we're going to have to go on an investigation of our own then."

"Halloween is just around the corner. I'm sure I'll be able to find some place that's haunted that we can check out."

True to her word, the next day she scoured the newspapers and Internet trying to find a ghost hunt she and Alex could go on. She saw several, but nothing called out to her. Just as she was ready to give up, she stumbled across an advertisement for a ghost hunt at an old Victorian mansion in southern Vermont. At first she dismissed it; it was a long drive. But something tugged at her as she studied the ad. It showed a large, imposing home with a turreted tower to one side, a gable on the other, a wraparound porch, and the most striking feature of all, a huge round window on the second floor above the porch. There was an intricately decorated black wrought iron fence in front of the home.

If this place isn't haunted, it should be, she mused as she took in the rather spooky-looking edifice.

The more she stared at the photo, the more she knew this was the place she and Alex needed to visit.

She opened up her web browser to do some research on the mansion, but a strong feeling in the pit of her stomach made her stop with her hands poised over the keyboard. Listening to that compelling gut feeling, she intuitively felt it was important to keep an open mind about the place without her emotions being compromised by whatever she might find out about its history. Whatever she and Alex felt when they arrived, if they felt anything at all, must remain pure from any preconceived notions. All she knew was that the large Victorian style house was named The Astoria after the family who had originally built it in 1888. Because of its age, the ghost hunt was being put on by a local group in hopes of raising enough money to save the mansion from falling apart.

What particularly caught her eye was the chance of attending a séance that would occur later on in the evening. She'd never been to one and, to her knowledge, neither had Alex. Even if there was nothing to experience in the mansion itself, they could at least be part of something she'd only read about in books. It was extra money to attend the séance, but it might be worth it.

Sitting back in her chair, Zoey absently brushed a strand of black hair from her face, her features deep in pensive concentration. Then, in an abrupt motion, she leaned forward, clicked the button 'Buy Here" and purchased tickets for her and Alex.

Well, she thought to herself, *we're committed now. Let's hope we find what we're looking for.*

On the night before Halloween, Zoey and Alex made the two-and-a-half-hour trip to The Astoria. Nestled in the countryside just outside one of the border towns between Vermont and Massachusetts, they drove through rolling farmland and up a hill that offered a beautiful view of Vermont's mountains. To their surprise, they found a sizeable crowd milling about outside the wrought iron fence that surrounded the mansion. Lanterns were hung on the fence, and the house itself was brightly lit. All in all, it had more of a party atmosphere than a serious ghost hunt.

"Wow, looks like we're not the only ones hoping to interact with the other side," Zoey quipped as she managed to park her car in one of the last available spots on the wide expanse of lawn next to the imposing mansion.

Mingling with the crowd, they immediately noticed that several people held tape recorders, cameras, and a K2 EMF meter, a small device with several small light bulbs over a spectrum of different colors. Having watched all the ghost shows, Zoey and Alex knew exactly what the equipment was for.

The K2 EMF meter was used to measure fluctuations in electromagnetic fields. The lights would go off whenever a ghost manipulated those fields in order to communicate with the living. The tape recorder was used to capture EVPs—electronic voice phenomena. Zoey didn't understand the science behind it, but somehow these small tape recorders had the ability to capture words or phrases uttered by a ghost.

Being empty-handed, she felt conspicuous. When she mentioned this to Alex, he replied, "We have something equally useful. We have our empathic abilities." He smiled impishly.

The night was cold, and being up on a hill with the wind blowing made the night feel even colder. Shivering in her coat, Zoey glanced at her watch. They had five minutes before the doors opened.

All around them, people murmured about what they hoped to experience in The Astoria. Both Zoey and Alex tried not to listen; they didn't want to know the history of the place. However, they had no choice when a loud voice directly behind them erupted in anger. Before she could stop herself, Zoey turned to see a short, overweight man in his mid-thirties, sporting a black goatee and long hair pulled back into a ponytail. He was clearly agitated as he flung his arms about in an effort to make his point with the small group he was with.

"I'm telling you, old man Astoria molested his daughter. It's well documented. That's why his wife killed herself and why he's still hanging around. He's consumed with guilt, as he should be."

"It's not well documented. That's just rumor," one of the girls in his group said.

"Oh yeah? Then why does everybody know about it? You can't keep stuff like that secret forever. Besides, there's no other reason for his wife taking her life."

"Did you ever think it's because she lost her daughter in that carriage accident, and she couldn't get over it?"

"Then why did he commit suicide?"

The girl sighed. "Jeez, Todd. Mr. Astoria didn't commit suicide. *That* is in the records. He died of a heart attack. If you ask me, after losing his only child and wife within a week of each other, I'd say he died of a broken heart."

"Bull. It's in all the stories about this place. They should just let this place go to ruin. Maybe that will wipe out the sins of what happened here."

"So much for not wanting to know the mansion's history," Zoey muttered under her breath in mild disgust.

"We don't know if what the guy is saying is true," Alex answered. "Just stay present and in the moment. I've noticed in the past that when I do that, my sensitivity and vibration increases. That will allow the energy to talk to us and really let us know what's going on here."

They agreed that was the best thing to do. A moment later, the wide oak doors to the mansion swung open and a middle aged woman with short, dark brown hair walked down the cement steps and opened the wrought iron fence. Once the crowd was through, she closed the gate and stepped back onto the front step, raising her arms to get everyone's attention. She was dressed in jeans and an oversize T-shirt with the name "The Paranormal Eye to the Other Side Investigative Team" blazoned on the front, with a picture of a huge eye staring out at the crowd. Stepping out from the mansion and arraying themselves behind her were three men ranging in ages from mid-twenties to mid-fifties. They also wore jeans and the requisite T-shirt with the huge eye and logo.

"Thank you all for coming," the woman announced. "My name is Sue and these are my fellow team members Robby, Joe, and Phil. Tonight promises to be a very active night. Therefore, in order for all of you to get the most out of your visit, we've decided to break you all down into smaller groups that will be led by one of us. If you don't want a guided tour of the house, you're free to wander around on your own. Just make sure to watch your step. As you can see, this place is old and in need of repair. We don't want any accidents. For those of you who paid extra for the séance, that will be starting in the parlor, which will be right in front of you when you enter, promptly at nine. You must be at the parlor at nine. Once the parlor doors close, you won't be able to get in. The séance will be led by Samantha Johnston. She's a very respected psychic who has worked with several local paranormal teams, including our own."

As the crowd shuffled towards the front door to be divided up amongst the paranormal team, Zoey turned to Alex. "You want a guide?"

Alex looked up at the imposing façade of the mansion. "Nope. I'd rather you and I just walk around. I think we'll have a better chance of feeling something without everyone else's energy mucking up the works. For most, it's hard to separate the energies of human excitement from the core energies of what's going on here."

Entering the foyer, the two were struck by a strong musty smell. The wallpapered walls had gouges here and there, and the green rug beneath their feet was heavily stained. Beneath the years of neglect, however, it was still possible to see the original molding around the ceilings speaking of wealth and taste of centuries past. Just as Sue had said, in front of them were two large wooden doors that rolled back to reveal a fire-placed parlor. There was already a long table set up with chairs around it, awaiting the time when it would host the séance.

To the right was a beautifully carved balustrade that curved up a winding set of wide stairs. While people milled about in the foyer, Alex pulled Zoey towards the stairs. "Let's start on the top floor and work our way down."

The two companions climbed the stairs. Halfway up, they were both stopped in their tracks by a loud male voice ringing in their ears.

"GET OUT!"

Zoey's eyes widened in surprise as she turned to Alex. "Did you hear that?"

"Yes. Somebody just yelled 'get out'."

"It's weird. I think I heard the voice from inside my head."

They both turned and looked down the stairs at the crowd still milling about in the foyer. "I did too," Alex said. "It's obvious no one else heard it, or else they'd be running up here with cameras, EVP recorders, and EMF meters."

"Do you think that was Mr. Astoria?"

"Don't know. But whoever it is obviously isn't happy that we and everybody else are in this house."

"Okay, I'm officially freaked out now."

Alex gave her a reassuring smile. "Repeat to yourself these are lessons in energy and empathy." He paused, then his grin widened. "You have to admit though, that was pretty cool."

"I'll admit that when I'm home safe and sound in my bed." She looked about her. "Maybe that Todd fellow was right. Maybe whoever just yelled at us doesn't want his secrets revealed."

"Remember what we agreed on. Keep an open mind and don't let what Todd or anyone else says influence what you feel."

Zoey took a deep breath and continued climbing the stairs. They reached the second-floor landing where, on either side of them, long corridors loomed out into the gloomy darkness. The walls were wallpapered with flowery patterns, the old fashioned gas lamps had been replaced with more modern fixtures, and the ceilings were decorated with ornate molding.

"I'm guessing this is where the family bedrooms are," Zoey replied.

"Then upstairs must be the servants quarters," Alex said. "We may get a few minutes of privacy before one of the tour groups shows up."

The two hurried on. Upstairs, the décor was vastly different from the second floor. The walls and ceiling were bare, and the hallway itself was lit by bare bulbs hanging from the ceiling. All around them were indications of restoration work in progress, with scaffolding and wide two-by-four planks lined up against the walls. The scratched and well-worn wooden floor was littered with plaster dust.

"Let's go to the right," Alex announced.

They gingerly made their way through the dust and grime, ending up at an empty room at the end of the corridor. The ceiling in the room was slanted, and it looked big enough to accommodate at least two twin beds.

"Close your eyes and just try to get a feel for the room," Alex instructed.

The two stood close to each other and closed their eyes. At first they felt nothing, but gradually, they both had the strongest sensation of someone walking down the corridor towards them. Zoey's heart began to beat faster and she blinked open her eyes.

"What the hell—" she whispered. Alex opened his eyes and she pointed down the corridor they had just walked up.

The two watched in amazement as a large, blue basketball-sized orb danced down the hallway towards them.

"What the heck is that?" she whispered as it moved past them. "It can't be dust, can it?"

"Not unless dust is blue," Alex responded.

Mesmerized, they watched as the orb went straight to a closed door in the center of the room and disappeared.

"What do we do?" Zoey whispered, even though they were alone.

"Well, we can run like hell or we can experience what's here and open the door." He gave her a direct look. "I say we open the door."

"You first," she said as she stepped behind him.

Alex stepped forward and, turning the knob, flung open the door. They peered inside and at first all they saw was a tiny closet hemmed in under the eaves. Then, imperceptibly at first, they began to see the shimmering of something moving. Was it the air disturbing the dust motes? Was it their imaginations?

Transfixed, they watched incredulously as a shadow emerged from the closet. Zoey unconsciously held her breath as it seemed to waver before them. Then, in an instant, it was gone.

"Please tell me you just saw a shadow person," Zoey replied. "Please!"

"I did," Alex concurred.

"Why was it hiding in the closet?"

"Wouldn't you if your home was invaded by dozens of people demanding a picture or an EVP or having their meters manipulated by you?"

"You've got a point."

The sound of climbing footsteps disturbed the silence. A moment later one of the tour groups appeared at the top of the stairs. Zoey and Alex unobtrusively made their way through the crowd and started down to the second floor.

"Did you feel anything when the shadow appeared?" Alex asked.

"I felt anxious and agitated," Zoey replied. "How about you?"

"Same here."

They tried to explore the second-floor bedrooms, but one of the tour groups was there already, snapping pictures, talking into their recorders and filling the air with their own expectant energy of seeing a ghost.

"No opportunity to experience energy here," Alex whispered to Zoey. "Too much human drama."

They had no choice but to retreat back to the ground floor.

To their relief, they found the ground floor empty. They meandered into what turned out to be the library, which still retained its masculine flavor with its dark wood paneling. An oil painting was hung on the wall above the fireplace that showed a stern-looking, middle aged man dressed in Victorian clothing. His dark hair and mutton chops were flecked with gray and his eyes seemed to eerily follow them as they moved through the room.

"I wonder if that's Mr. Astoria himself," Zoey asked as they stood beneath the painting. "He sure doesn't look like the friendliest of people."

Alex didn't say anything. When she turned to see if he'd heard her, she noticed his features furrowed in deep concentration. After a few moments, he shook his head as if to clear it.

"For a minute, I felt as though I was back with Mr. Astoria," Alex replied slowly. "It's the same feeling I had back in Tombstone, as though I'm straddling two time periods." Alex looked up at the portrait. "He was a tough, yet fair, businessman. I feel that energy. But as to what Todd said outside about him and his daughter . . ." Alex shook his head again. "I'm just not feeling it. I would expect to feel guilt or remorse if the story was true. Instead, I feel his outrage that such a story is being said about him."

"Maybe we'll find out more during the séance."

"Let's take a break outside and try to clear ourselves."

A half-hour later, Zoey and Alex found themselves seated at the table in the parlor. The psychic, Samantha Johnston, was a large woman with a protruding belly and a mass of very bright red/orange hair. She was dressed in a boldly colored caftan and Zoey wondered if her looks were more for effect than for anything else. Her outfit certainly made her stand out. Next to her sat Sue, the woman who had greeted them at the start of the investigation. To her dismay, just as they were about to close the doors and start the séance, Todd and his female companion swept in.

"Thank God we made it. Don't want to miss this." He sat down across from Zoey and Alex. Zoey couldn't quite understand why, but her stomach instantly tightened and she started to get a bad feeling. Before she could whisper her concerns to Alex, Samantha began to speak.

"We're going to open a doorway between the dimension of the living and the dimension of the dead. It's vital that once we begin this circle, we do not, under any circumstances, break it. I'm, therefore, going to ask you all to join hands while I light this white candle and say a prayer of protection. Sue, could you please turn down the lights?"

Sue dimmed the lights, but not enough that the participants couldn't see each other. After lighting the long tapered candle that stood on the table in front of her, Samantha began intoning a prayer.

"We call in our guides and ask that they watch over us and protect us, allowing only those spirits in who wish to communicate with us." As she continued in the same vein, Zoey glanced sideways at Alex. She knew how he felt about protection prayers. The only true protection was to remove whatever vulnerabilities a person carried by healing them. This removed anything a spirit could attach to. To his credit, Alex kept his face neutral. She turned her attention back to Samantha.

"We now invite any spirits who wish to speak with us to enter our circle of love and light. We wish you no harm. We only wish to communicate with you this evening. This is your opportunity to speak."

Zoey surreptitiously peeked out at the attendees. Many of the expressions were that of hopeful anticipation. A few were skeptical. However, Todd had what could only be described as a look of disgust marring his features. Once again she felt her stomach tighten and she unconsciously held her breath.

"There is nothing to fear from us. We wish to acknowledge your existence. Please join us."

Suddenly, Zoey and Alex felt an energy begin to build. Gradually, steadily, it filled the room, slowly moving from one person to the other. Around and around the table it went. The energy had a masculine flavor to it, and Zoey thought she smelled the faint aroma of cigar smoke. She quickly noticed the room grow colder as the energy grew heavier. She and Alex exchanged glances. He felt it, too. Both were having a hard time with the energy as it continued to increase, a barely contained aura of aggressive unpredictability underlying it. She looked to Samantha and was surprised to find that instead of reacting to the dread that was building in her own stomach, the psychic appeared unaffected. In fact, she was smiling.

No empath there, she thought to herself as she took in Samantha's energy and facial features. *Surely if she was even the least bit sensitive, she'd be feeling this heavy energy.*

"I feel the presence of Mr. Astoria," Samantha said, her eyes closed, her body slightly swaying back and forth. "We welcome you into our circle. We wish to help you in any way we can."

Zoey turned her head and tried not to gasp as she saw a shimmering in the air, reminiscent of the energy she'd seen upstairs in the closet. Would she see the blue orb again? Or was it possible that Mr. Astoria was actually going to materialize? Was she actually going to see her first ghost? Maybe there really was something to these séances.

Silence fell over the room as anticipation and a nervousness from several at the table started to grow. The energy now zipped around the table as the shimmering continued, not quite materializing, but nevertheless noticeable in the semi-darkness.

"Please step forward, Mr. Astoria," Samantha said. "There is nothing to be afraid of. We're here to help you."

The energy now seemed to zip even faster around the participants. The temperature grew colder. The sense of deep anxiety increased. Zoey was both terrified and fascinated.

The energy continued to build. Something was about to happen. But what?

"Why the hell should we help that jerk?" Todd suddenly yelled out, the venom in his voice shattering the concentration of the group. "He deserves to be stuck in hell!"

"NOOOOOOOOOO!" wailed an unbidden voice.

The energy exploded.

Before anyone knew what was happening, Todd was hurled from his chair and physically thrown to the floor.

Several people tumbled from their chairs, screaming in terror as they tried to get as far away from the table and Todd as they could.

"Stop! Keep the contact!" Samantha yelled out as she too jumped to her feet and tried to regain control. But it was no use. The few who had jumped up were now backed against the wall, jabbering nervously as they tried to calm their trembling limbs. It was left to Zoey and Alex to help Todd to his feet.

"What the hell happened?" Todd seethed as he glared about him.

"Looks like you ticked off Mr. Astoria," Alex replied.

Embarrassed and angered by what had happened, Todd shook off Alex's hand.

The emotional energy threatened to get out of hand as fear built upon fear. In that moment, Alex knew that as empaths, he and Zoey needed to change the energy of the room. It was obvious to him that Samantha, coming from a place of only what she could see rather than what she could feel, lacked the ability to calm the energy down.

"Why don't we all return to our seats?" Alex said to the participants.

There was something in his voice—a calmness and authority—that compelled everyone to do as he asked.

"I'd like to say something," Alex replied. Without waiting for permission, he closed his eyes and started to speak.

"Let us all begin to breathe deeply. Feel the place within you where you're calm. Where a truth and a light resides. Where there is no judgment. Where those places within you and without you know that everything is as it needs to be. As that unfolds, we ask that this space and those within this space begin to realize that we are here as an example. We are here not to judge. We are here not to blame. We are just here as a collection, a knowing of light. Present in a peaceful state. Just as we are in that peaceful state, we ask the same of the beings that reside within this room, within this house. As we are forgiven, know you too are forgiven."

Whether it was his words or his still, peaceful energy, a calmness now filled the room as the group silently listened to his words. When he was done, he opened his eyes and looked to Samantha. Although her face was white, she immediately strove to reassert control.

"I think we've all had enough for this evening. I now close this circle and ask that our guides continue to protect us."

Zoey leaned over to Alex and whispered, "If I was Samantha, I'd revisit those protection prayers. They didn't seem to do much good."

Arising from their chairs and turning to leave, Samantha called out to Alex. "Where did you learn how to do that?" she asked.

"This is the first time I've ever done it."

Her eyes widened. "Impossible!"

He shrugged. "It seemed like the right thing to do. I've been in situations before where things have gotten out of hand and the only thing that brings them back into focus is when someone can project an energy of peacefulness into the room. It's part of what I've been trying to understand all my life. It's why I'm here tonight." He gazed steadily at her. "I'm an empath. I feel everything."

SITTING IN JUDGMENT

As we know all too well, human beings are quick to judge. As an empath, ninety percent of what we feel and makes us feel uncomfortable is the judgment of others. Even in that where we begin to judge the energy we're feeling, our own energy follows suit. It's a cat and mouse game to find that place within us that feels balanced and light.

Death itself is the great unknown. There are so many judgments of what exactly happens after we cease to physically exist. More times than not, that innate curiosity turns to fear. It is especially fearful when it comes to the idea of hauntings—the thought of someone who is stuck between the realm of the living and the realm of the dead. Compounding this fear is the religious teachings of sin. Does the wandering in the afterlife have anything to do with sin? What sort of penance needs to be undertaken in order to move on? Do the living contribute to this wandering in some way? Like Todd in the above story, was his need to be better than Mr. Astoria, to sit in judgment of what he perceived Mr. Astoria's sin to be contributing to the inability of the spirit to move on? Or was Mr. Astoria's need to declare his innocence holding him back? Is it possible that some of the wanderers are here because of their own thoughts of grief or guilt? Whatever the reason, empaths feel the emotions of the dead just as much as they feel the emotions of the living. Maybe it's up to us to find ways to change the energy of a situation because in so doing, we have the ability to bring Light to the afterlife.

As to the blue orb: There have been many discussions, many photos of orbs. Some can be dismissed as dust motes or insects. However, there are some that cannot be so easily explained away. We're not quite sure what they are, but they seem to hold some kind of energetic knowledge—a thought, a spirit, a moment in time, culminating in some kind of physical experience that manifests in front of someone who is sensitive. The jury is still out, but you can be sure that our energetic curiosity will keep us looking into what orbs are and why they exist.

The holidays came and went

The holidays came and went. The curiosity to understand what had happened at The Astoria, however, remained unabated. What had the blue orb been trying to tell them? Why had Todd been attacked? Was it simply because he'd insulted old man Astoria? Or was there more to it?

By February, Zoey was more than ready to continue her explorations into the relationship between the living and the dead. She was joined by another of Alex's students who was also eager to comprehend what these shadow people were, since she too had begun to see them.

Nell was a nurse who continually found herself becoming increasingly exhausted as she tended to the sick at the hospital where she worked. Many times she physically felt the pain her patients were experiencing. It helped her ease their discomfort, but did nothing to replenish her own spent energy. Hearing about Alex through friends, she went to one of his classes and immediately recognized herself as an empath. She became friendly with Zoey and spent many hours discussing what she was going through, including the new phenomena, at least for her, of seeing shadows darting about a patient's room, especially if they were on the brink of dying.

"I've heard about loved ones who have already died coming to be there when it's their relative's time to pass," Nell told Zoey one day. "I'm beginning to think that may be what I'm seeing."

Zoey agreed.

In keeping with that thought, the next time Zoey saw Alex, she told him of her idea. "We need more experiences in order to figure this ghost stuff out, correct?"

"Yes," Alex answered.

"Then what do you say to visiting America's most haunted site?"

"Which is?"

"Gettysburg National Park in Pennyslvania. I was watching a program on it and the narrator said the battlefield has the reputation of being the most haunted—" Zoey stopped when she saw Alex's face blanch. "Are you okay?"

He offered her a sheepish shrug. "Well, to be honest, I've always been terrified of going to Gettysburg."

"Why?"

Alex shook his head. "I'm not sure. But whenever it's been brought up, I freeze. I just don't like the idea of going there."

Zoey fixed him with a steady eye. "Then isn't it time you face your fears head on? In all the years I've known you, I've never seen you shy away from anything. In fact, I've never heard you say you don't like something."

"True."

"Then come on, it'll be fun. You, Nell, and I will go for a long weekend. How bad can it be?"

Alex would have cause to remember those words as they stepped out of the car onto the snow-covered field that made up part of the Gettysburg National Military Park.

The small town of Gettysburg, Pennsylvania, was the site of a pivotal battle during the American Civil War. Fought July 1st through the 3rd in 1863, the battle involved the largest number of casualties of the entire war and effectively ended General Robert E. Lee and the Confederate forces' attempt to invade the North.

The air was cold and biting, the skies gray and overcast, the battlefield deserted of tourists on that wintry February afternoon as the three friends stepped out of the car. All around them the landscape was dotted with statues of different shapes and sizes, each honoring the many states and their battalions that had fought there more than a century before. Zoey turned to say something to Alex, but caught herself when she saw the expression on his face. He looked stricken. Concerned he was ill, she hurried to his side. "What's wrong? Are you all right?"

"Don't talk to me."

She stood a step back, startled by his uncharacteristic brusqueness. She and Nell exchanged concerned looks.

Despite all the situations Alex had found himself in throughout his life dealing with all sorts of energies, both good and bad, he'd never felt *completely* overwhelmed as he did now. This was worse than Arizona, worse than The Astoria, worse than Tombstone. He felt as though he were in the midst of a swarm of bees buzzing around him. Within him. Inside his very brain. He didn't know where he started or ended. It was as if he were a giant blackboard with hundreds of jumbled words scrawled all over it, not making sense, but demanding to be made sense of. There were so many emotions enveloping him, it took all his willpower not to start screaming in an effort to make it all go away.

He had to get back to basics. He couldn't plug into all he was feeling or he would truly go mad. He took a few deep breaths of cold, winter air and tried his best to ground.

Stay focused. Don't give into what you're feeling, he repeated over and over to himself.

He took one step. Then another. He turned his eye toward a statue in front of him. It was of a bare-headed, uniformed man on horseback. The bronze figure had his hand on his sword and his gaze was directed across a huge field that lay in front of him.

Forcing himself to look at the placard, Alex saw the name George Meade emblazoned on it. Alex knew he'd been the general in charge of the Union Army during the battle. By deliberately keeping his focus on the statue, he found the frenzied energies begin to recede. As in many times in his empathic life, focusing on an object brought him back to a place of knowing where his energy began and ended.

Zoey, who was keeping a sharp eye on him, felt his energy calm. She came up to him and rested her hand on his arm.

"You okay now?"

He nodded. "I felt as though I were drowning."

"I could feel something was going on with you. The energy here is crazy. We can go back to the hotel and get a fresh start tomorrow morning."

"No. I need to figure out what just happened." He pointed to a hill that lay behind the statue of General Meade. "Let's go up there. There's something about that hill that's drawing me to it."

They climbed back into the car and as Nell drove towards the hill, Zoey read aloud from her guidebook.

"The outcropping of granite boulders over to our right is known as Devil's Den. Confederate sharpshooters used this spot to pick off Union soldiers further up at a place called Little Round Top. It says here that during the summer months, no matter how hot the day gets, it's always cool and damp between the rocks. Apparently there are several ghosts at Devil's Den and Little Round Top that tourists have reported seeing."

"There is something all over this place," Alex murmured as they drew closer to Little Round Top.

Getting out of the car and walking down a well-worn path, they found themselves on a huge outcropping of granite that gave them a commanding view of the entire battlefield. It was breathtaking, and the three stood there silently, taking everything in. Once again, he had to focus very intensely on not getting caught up in the confusion of all he was feeling. He had to take a step back and systematically make sense of what he was going through.

Suddenly, Nell gave a start.

"Oh my God. Do you hear that?"

Zoey and Alex paused for a moment and closed their eyes. It didn't take long before they began to hear whispers on the cold breeze of men yelling and cannons going off. In the next moment all three jumped as they felt the distinct sensation of something icy physically walking *through* them, followed by the unmistakable odor of stale sweat.

"Oh my God!" Nell repeated. "What the hell just happened?" She yelped and suddenly grabbed her head. "I just felt something crash into my head!"

As her emotions escalated, Alex came up to her and laid a reassuring hand on her shoulder. "You've got to do what I did, Nell. Just focus on something and don't give in to what you're feeling. Take a deep breath and let it out slowly. Now take another. Just allow the experience to unfold."

Nell did as he asked. After a few minutes, her heart stopped racing.

"What was that about?" she whispered.

"There's so much horror that happened here. I think it's left a scar in time," Alex explained. "I believe that because of our empathy, we're feeling and experiencing the energy of what the soldiers went through. I have no other explanation."

"When you consider how many men fought and died here, no wonder it's so overwhelming," Zoey replied. "So much emotion. So much energy of emotion. It's as if it's burnt into the very air."

"But what was that icy cold that went through all of us?" Nell asked.

Alex took his time answering. "I believe we felt soldiers walking through us. That would also explain the sweat we smelled."

"Is it the trauma that's keeping them all here?" Zoey asked. "Do they know they are even here?"

Alex looked out over the field. "Yes. But there's something more. I'm just not quite sure what it is yet."

With nighttime approaching, they decided to go to their hotel and settle in for the night.

The next morning found the trio driving to the other side of the huge flat field where the start of the infamous Pickett's Charge took place.

On the last day of the battle, with General Lee determined to break through the center of the Union's forces, he had his men march across a wide-open field. The charge was futile; the Confederate troops suffered a fifty percent casualty rate.

They parked near a statue of another horsed officer—this time Robert E. Lee—and looked across the meadow towards where they'd stood the day before.

"Can you imagine the courage it must have taken to walk across this field with the Union's cannons exploding all around you?" Zoey marveled as she looked at the fences that intersected the area.

"How does the energy feel to you right now?" Alex asked.

The two women stood silent for a moment, absorbing the energies around them. "There's so much sadness here. So much regret," Zoey concluded.

"Right. Now let's go back to the Union side of the battlefield."

Knowing Alex was on to something, the ladies climbed back into the car and ten minutes later they were once again standing at Little Round Top. "Now what do you feel?" Alex asked.

"It's lighter here. Certainly lighter than yesterday. I'm not feeling the sadness I felt over at Pickett's Charge," Nell replied.

"This seems to be the side with most of the ghostly activity," Zoey added. "Why do you think that is?"

"I'm working on a theory. The next stop is the graveyard where President Lincoln gave his famous Gettysburg Address."

"Wait a minute," Nell spoke up. "Aren't we supposed to be gathering evidence? I haven't done any EVP sessions or taken many pictures."

"This is more a trip of exploration rather than evidence gathering," Alex answered her. "I just want you to really think about what you're feeling as we visit the different locations here."

Climbing into the car, it was a five-minute ride to the graveyard.

They gathered in front of a marble wall. On each side of the wall was a stone pillar. In the center was a bust of Lincoln. On either side of the bust were two plaques that held the 272-word speech that began with the stirring words, "Fourscore and seven years ago our fathers brought forth, on this continent, a new nation, conceived in liberty, and dedicated to the proposition that all men are created equal."

"If I remember my class on American History," Alex said, "this speech served to remind the public just what the war they were suffering for was all about."

They read the speech, the words causing a shudder to move through them. Nell sat down on a nearby bench and took a deep breath.

"There's so much here," she admitted. "I think I need a break."

"We can go the visitor center," Zoey offered. "To tell the truth, we all need a break."

They once more climbed into their vehicle and drove the short distance to the huge visitor center. There was a museum with exhibits of actual items owned by both Union and Confederate soldiers, as well as the townspeople, alongside an enormous bookstore and souvenir shop. Deciding to leave the museum for last, they wandered into the bookstore. In one corner, a television mounted on the wall was showing a scene from the 1993 film *Gettysburg*.

Drawing her attention, Zoey realized what she was seeing was the film's reenactment of the courageous, but ultimately doomed, Pickett's Charge.

She couldn't tear her eyes from the screen as cannon balls exploded in a plume of dirt and blood all around the soldiers. She watched men screaming in agony as they were hit, going down in a pool of blood as their comrades stepped over their dying bodies and continued the hopeless march. Suddenly and unexpectedly, she felt a coldness inside her—the same coldness she'd felt up on Little Round Top. She felt the unmistakable tingling around her shoulder blades and knew in that instant there were spirits surrounding her. Before she could fully comprehend what was happening, her eyes stung with tears and she started to sob.

"Are you all right?" she heard at her elbow. She saw Alex out of the corner of her eye. She held up her hand. She couldn't answer. Her throat was swollen with too much emotion. He watched her for a few moments, then gently putting his arm around her, led her outside. Cleaning off the snow from a marble bench, they sat down side by side. The chilly February air worked its way through Zoey's distress and she was finally able to take a deep, steadying breath.

"No wonder you never wanted to come here," she sniffled. "I've never had the kinds of experiences I've had here." She looked at him, her eyes still brimming with tears. "I don't know why I started to cry like that. It isn't like I've never seen that movie before. But here—today—" She paused. "Have you figured it out yet?"

He nodded. "I think I'm getting closer to the answer."

ENERGY

As an empath, it's very hard to get to a place where you understand where your own energy begins and ends. That's why, in highly charged emotional moments, the energies of whatever happened begin to overwhelm. It's as if our very body is reacting to what is around us, not only physically but in the inability to clear our thoughts or clear the fidgety anxiety that something is about to happen. We're being filled with some kind of vibrational swamp that doesn't belong to us. Some of the skills empaths learn to get back to a centered space include grounding, moving the energy through you and out of you, much the way trees take in carbon dioxide and release oxygen. One of the most talked about skills empaths use is shielding themselves so no energy can come through you and affect you. Sometimes this works. But as we explained in our book, The Reluctant Empath, it only works for so long. Energy still demands to be experienced. The more you shield, the more you attract energy to yourself that you believe you need to shield yourself from. However, is it possible that shielding is not truly the gift and skill of an empath, but more of a knee-jerk reaction to what you perceive as good or bad energy? Is it possible that experiencing the energy and learning to be okay with it and changing its vibration is really what being an empath is all about? Imagine walking into a space and every thought and every feeling begins to stick to you, like a blackboard filled with jumbled words, incoherent thoughts, runaway emotions. This is the experience of many empaths. Yet, is there a way to make sense of how the words on the blackboard align? Is there a way to create a story of what is there?

There's a lot of information in the energy that surrounds us. Think about the thousands of tourists who visit Gettysburg and similar historical sites. In particular, think about the reenactors who relive what occurred in any given space. They may not be able to recreate the blood and trauma, but the intention and thought of that purpose leaves that energy there. Perhaps this is why sites such as Gettysburg are filled with the paranormal. The soldiers who remain there experience once again what happened to them year after year on the anniversary that reenactors and the public celebrate. All this information, all this energy needs to be unwoven or rearranged. As an empath, you are able to do it. But first, you must know where your own energy begins and ends. You don't want to find yourself in a situation like Zoey's, where she was so distraught watching the reenactment of Pickett's Charge because she was feeling what the soldiers who died in that battle were feeling. Or Alex and Nell, when they felt they were ready to explode from all the crazy energy they were feeling. The ability to focus on an object allows you to not be as affected by the energy around you because your energy begins to flow into singlemindedness. Focusing allows your mind to calm, much the way rosary beads, worry beads, or prayer beads do. As you find yourself easing back to a space of calm, you can now start to slowly open up to your experiences and begin to discern and unravel the emotions of the moment. Your body gives you clues. Your thoughts give you clues. Your feelings give you clues. The site you're in gives you clues. All that energy now begins to tell a story. Once you begin to see the story, you can now begin to add a sense of calm to the situation. To actually change the energy that's there. We believe this is part of being an empath. This is part of your gift.

That night at dinner

That night at dinner, the trio went over the events of the day.

"We've only been here a day and a half, and I can't believe all we've been through already," Nell admitted. "With all that energy coming at me, I thought I'd explode."

"There seems to be a recurring theme to our experiences as empaths," Alex said. "As long as we don't plug into what we're feeling—ride the wave of the emotions, so to speak—it doesn't stick to us." He turned to Nell. "Isn't that what happened when I told you to focus on something other than what you were feeling?"

She nodded. "The overwhelming feelings slipped away quickly."

"So what is your explanation for what went on today? I know you've been thinking about it," Zoey asked Alex.

Alex smiled. "I have." He slowly sat back in his chair. "This place is bound to affect anyone who's even the slightest bit sensitive. But for those of us who have fully embraced our empathy, it's completely over the top. Why? Because it's not only place memory that's here, but countless spirits that haven't left. Mix in the energy of the visitors, and you have a pea soup of feeling."

Nell held up her hand. "You mentioned that term yesterday. What exactly is place memory?"

"It's an event or a series of events that are literally burned into space and time. The trauma of what happened here—the suffering, the anguish, the dying, the sheer terror of being shot at or blown apart by cannon, the will to survive—that's going to sear itself into the fabric of time. I'm convinced we tapped into that as soon as we got out of the car." He took a sip of his ginger ale. "There were a series of skirmishes fought here over three days, ending with the bloodbath known as Pickett's Charge. The energy we've felt since we arrived here reflects the confusion of what those men experienced. I couldn't keep straight what I was feeling. It was as though I kept getting pulled under a giant wave of haphazard energies." He looked at Nell. "I've been thinking about that pain you suddenly felt in your head. I believe what you felt was a soldier being shot in the head."

Nell's eyes widened. "Really?"

"It makes sense. When we were at the OK Corral, Zoey had a similar experience. She felt a sudden pain in her wrist. Time as we know it doesn't truly exist. For someone as empathic as you are, it's very easy, especially in a place like this, to walk through a space where something traumatic occurred and feel it as though it's happening again. There were hundreds of casualties up on Little Round Top. You walked through a space where a soldier was shot in the head. For that second, you transcended time and space and felt what he felt. Zoey, you walked through the spot where Billy Clanton got shot in the wrist. Because of your empathic abilities, you felt what happened to him at that very moment."

"So basically we actually felt those soldiers running through us up there?" Nell asked, her face awestruck by the thought.

"Yes. We felt their energy. We experienced their fear. We smelled their sweat. How many times have you heard a particular song and been transported back to a memory where that song was played? The same thing happened up at Little Round Top. We were transported back to that moment when the battle was taking place. We heard their battle cries and the explosion of cannon fire. Anyone who is empathic and walks through there will feel it. How can they not? This place is crazy! The experiences of those soldiers are seared into the fabric of time all over this area. It's the same as when a living person reacts in fear or anger. We feel that, correct? Well, we're feeling the instant trauma that was left here as well.

"Now think about what we felt when we were on the opposing side of the Pickett's Charge field. When we were on the Northern side, we felt, not only that place memory, but the actual spirits of the men. The energy itself wasn't as sad and heavy as it was on the Southern side."

"That's because the Northern side won the battle of Gettysburg," Zoey pointed out.

"And the energy we were feeling reflects that. Although men died on both sides, the Union Army won the day, while the Confederates were defeated and ultimately lost the war."

"But that doesn't explain why there are more ghosts on the Northern side than the Southern side," Nell said.

"Let me ask you this." Alex leaned over, warming to the subject. "Do you remember which side had the most monuments? At least from our vantage point on the battlefield?"

Nell tilted her head. "Mmmm. Now that I think about it, I think the Northern side did."

Alex smiled. "Yes. Every battalion has a monument erected in its memory. The monument dedicated to Pennsylvania alone is an enormous tower. With the exception of the statue of Robert E. Lee on the battlefield, I can't remember any statues dedicated to the Confederacy that were as large or as prominent."

"What is your point?"

"It isn't the foot soldiers who make it into the history books. It's the generals, the officers who led them into battle. We hear about Meade, about Chamberlain, about Robert E. Lee, or Ulysses Grant. We don't hear about Joe Smith or Robert Jones who carried out their orders. If it weren't for these monuments, those foot soldiers wouldn't be remembered on such a large scale."

Nell frowned. "I'm not sure I follow you."

"History tells us that a number of the men who fought here were Irish immigrants. Back then, if a man could afford it, he could buy someone to take his place in the army. Many of the men who took their place were Irish immigrants just off the boats. They had no clue what they were fighting for. Suddenly, they find themselves here, trying their best to survive. There were also farmers, clerks, men who had never ventured out of their towns and villages until they went to war. In other words, they were nobodies who never would have been remembered except by family members or their names carved into forgotten gravestones. Yet here, they're somebody. Thousands of people flock here year after year to pay homage to the bravery of the men who fought here. They're remembered. They're honored. They aren't nobodies forgotten by history."

Comprehension spread over Nell's face. "They live off the energy of the living who come to pay their respects and honor what they did."

Alex grinned. "Exactly. They're honored here in a way they never would have been honored if they'd stayed at home and not gone to war."

Zoey's jaw dropped as a thought occurred to her. "Oh my God! Now I know what happened to me in the bookstore." She looked excitedly at her two companions.

"It isn't that there aren't any spirits on the Confederate side. Of course there are. They're honored just as the Union soldiers are by the people who flock here." She paused, trying to find the words to describe what she'd just realized. "We've done a lot of work to heal our issues. As we've healed, our vibration has increased. We're more open. We feel the soldiers more because of that heightened vibration. It helps us to be more aware of the energy around us. At the same time, the spirits are attracted to us because of our light. I felt tingles as soon as we left the battlefield and went to the visitors center. I now realize the tingles were the energy of spirits that followed me. When I turned my attention to the television and started watching the part of the movie that reenacted Pickett's Charge, it was as though those soldiers who had followed me were watching the movie through my eyes." She saw the puzzlement on Nell's face and added excitedly, "Don't you see? It's as if it was the *first time* they saw what happened to them. During the actual battle, they were too busy trying to stay alive and get across that field. But now, they saw for the first time the enormity of what they'd been a part of. They saw the futility of it all. They'd experienced the horror of it through me. And they cried. That's why I was so overcome with tears. I cried for them and with them."

Alex nodded. "I've also come to believe that when a person dies in a traumatic way, they may not even realize they're dead. That explains the anxiety we feel sometimes from spirit. Imagine trying to get your loved ones or anyone to speak to you but they can't because they can't even see you." Alex shook his head. "That would really be like a hell on earth."

Zoey leaned forward in her chair. "Something just occurred to me. Do you think the living also have a hand in keeping the dead here by not being able to let them go when a loved one dies? I've heard of people grieving for years. I wonder if that energy keeps the dead from moving on. It's as though the grief of the living bind the dead to them."

Alex nodded. "I agree. I believe that does happen. Now, I'm not saying a person shouldn't grieve when they've lost someone. But excessive grieving does have the potential of keeping a departed loved one bound to them. Maybe it's because the dead feel their loved ones grieving so much, they can't move on, or feel afraid to move on." He shook his head. "I don't think the living understand just how powerful their energy can be."

Nell sighed. "I have to tell you, this empathic stuff is a pain. How are we supposed to live our life? Does this mean that no matter where we go, we have to re-experience the energy that's left there?"

"Not if we don't judge what happened. Not if we don't plug into what we're feeling. Remember, when we add our judgments or fears or anxiety into the mix, we're only making the energy we feel worse. I think back to what happened at The Astoria. We didn't judge old man Astoria. We didn't add our energies to what was already there at the séance. Todd did. And look what happened to him. The important thing to remember is if we realize we're here to observe and allow the energies to move through us, we can get through it."

"You mean that grounding you told me about?" Nell asked.

"That's part of it. Yes, we can ground the energy. But our lives are made up of lessons. This whole battlefield is a perfect classroom to feel the different kinds of energies. We felt what was left behind, not only by the dead, but by the living as well. Year after year, people come here and leave the residue of their expectations, their beliefs over what happened here. An empath is going to feel all of that. No wonder it can be so overwhelming. Yet, if we approach each situation with the idea of what will this teach me, we can get through it easier. Does that make sense?"

Nell nodded. "I suppose so." She paused, then continued, "However, there must be a purpose besides learning a lesson. Once we learn the lesson, then what? There's a reason for a lesson. It's to teach us something we need to know. Why do we need to know about these different energies? Why do we care if the Northern side of this battlefield feels different than the Southern Side? Who cares that Zoey started to cry in front of a movie because the spirits saw how they died more than a hundred years after it happened?" She looked to each of her companions. "What is the point to all of this? And," she added before Alex could answer. "I understand why the soldiers stay here. But why does Mr. Astoria still haunt his house? Why are the prostitutes still at the Bird Cage Theater? Why do some spirits move on while others stay behind?"

Alex met her gaze. "I don't know yet. But I have a feeling we'll be finding out pretty soon."

BEING A LIGHT

There are so many stories about the afterlife where people needed to be transported or walked into a better place—whether it's the Ferryman over the river Styx, or the stories of departed loved ones coming to take a relative home at their moment of death. Is it possible that as an empath, as you develop your ability to become a light in a dark space, you in turn garner more attention from the spirits that are wandering in the darkness? You learn through healing and your own experiences how your energy works and how your vibration can be increased. You learn that as you peel off the blanket of heaviness and despair, you're lightening up the world around you. In this kind of thinking, is it possible that part of your experience is first, being okay with what you feel and secondly, understanding what you're feeling?

There is much thought about the process known as psycho-metry—the belief that objects hold energy. Many empaths are able to pick up an object and physically feel what its owner felt. Think about the crosses that are on the side of the road. As an empath drives by, many times they feel the energy of the person the cross is honoring. They may feel how the person died. The living direct energy towards that cross, just as the living direct energy towards departed loved ones, or at historical sites. Is it possible all this energy is contributing to keeping a spirit stuck?

In the same vein, because you are so sensitive to energy, you can drive past a certain house and feel something is off. Or drive on a highway and feel a shudder because it's the sight of a fatality. Is it the energy of the space or is a spirit calling out to you? This is part of what empathic people are starting to understand. Because of your ability to change energy, you will find yourself drawn to people, places, things, and not quite know why at first. Experiences then begin to happen. By staying open, the moment begins to build upon a body of empathic knowledge. You're there for a reason. Could it be the reason is for you to use your light, to use your heightened vibration and change the energy?

A note about place memory versus an actual haunting: This is a question we are asked many times. A place memory has no human emotion to it. It's like a scene in a movie that is played over and over again because, as we mentioned in the story above, it's a moment seared into the fabric of time. A haunting, however, is filled with human emotion. There's a presence of an actual spirit. You, as an empath, will feel the energy of that spirit.

WE'RE
SUPPOSED
TO HELP

After watching the television programs on ghost investigations, as well as experiencing what they did in Gettysburg, once they returned home Alex felt compelled to pull together his own paranormal investigative team. He had a feeling the answers he was seeking, especially in answer to the question Nell had asked about what the whole point was of what they were going through, would be found investigating homes where the occupants too were trying to figure out why they were being visited by the Other Side or why the spirits wouldn't leave.

Knowing Cora and Keri were too frightened to even think about dealing with the area of ghosts and hauntings, he instead turned to Zoey, Nell, and another of their friends to join them.

Ariel was an artist who specialized in abstract art. She'd met Alex through the usual means—having sensed others' emotions all her life and reaching a point where it was becoming difficult to venture out without being bombarded. She'd joined his workshops to get a handle on her empathy. She was completely open to whatever possibilities her spiritual path had to offer and she readily agreed to be part of his team. With her long brown hair and enormous green eyes, she was eager to explore the Other Side.

Naming his group The Spirit Light Network, Alex put up business cards whenever he could. He then set out ground rules for his team.

"Rule number one: No matter what happens, we remain calm. We don't plug into whatever we feel. Many times, these families are frightened; otherwise they wouldn't be calling us. We have to present a professional, calm demeanor or all hell could break lose. Rule number two: We don't ask what's going on up front. I think it would be beneficial for us, as empaths, to get a feel for the energy without having any preconceived ideas of what's going on. Rule number three: We don't judge the situation. Let the energy speak for itself."

They all agreed on these points and waited for their first investigation to happen. It wasn't long before Zoey received an excited phone call from Alex.

"We've got our first case," he exclaimed excitedly.

"Really?"

"Yes. They saw one of the cards I put out. I made a point of not asking what's going on, so we could really rely on the energy speaking to us. All I know is that the woman is frightened for herself and her children. I want us all to keep an open mind like we did at The Astoria. I'll call the rest of the group and see if they can make it Saturday night."

Of course, the others jumped at this opportunity and Saturday evening found the intrepid ghost hunters driving down the residential street of a seaside town looking for a specific address.

"Are we supposed to feel stuff even before we get to where we're going?" Ariel asked.

"Energy is energy. It doesn't follow the rules of time and distance," Alex replied. "Why?"

"I'm getting this wicked headache."

Zoey and Nell admitted they too were dealing with the sudden onslaught of a headache.

"And," Ariel continued, "I keep hearing the name 'Mitch'."

"I didn't ask for any details. So we'll just see what's going on when we get there."

They finally pulled in front of what is known as a three decker in New England. Basically, it was a three-story house with each apartment having its own small porch. Even in the dim light they could see the house had seen better days. The paint was peeling and there were toys strewn all over the small front yard.

Climbing out of the car into the cold night air, they went up the steps and Alex rang the doorbell. A moment later, a young, slim woman of average height with dark blonde hair answered the door. She was dressed in jeans and an oversized sweater. Although pretty, her features were marred with the signs of fatigue and exhaustion.

"Hi. I'm Alex."

"Thank you, thank you for coming," she said, the gratitude plainly evident in her voice. "You have no idea how much this means to us that you're here. I'm Patsy."

The group entered the cramped living room and introduced themselves. The furniture was worn and old, but Patsy kept a very neat house. A scented candle was lit, and they were greeted by a lovely gardenia aroma.

"My kids and husband are in the kitchen. Is it okay that my boys are here?" she asked as she led the way down a short corridor. The group looked at each other.

"Sure, why not?" Alex responded. "They're being affected by whatever is here."

They entered a small kitchen. At the scratched and battered kitchen table sat two young boys. There was a strong resemblance to Patsy as they gazed with great curiosity at Alex and his group. One looked to be eight years old, while the other looked to be around ten. Standing near the stove drinking from a beer can was a tall, thin man, with dark hair and a cautious smile.

"I'm Brian," he greeted as he shook everyone's hands. "Sure glad you guys could come out here tonight."

As soon as the group entered the kitchen, they all began to feel a tight clench in the pit of their stomachs. Anxiety pulsed through them and a pain started to build behind their eyes as they all looked at each other. Knowing their rule about not plugging in or creating any more drama, they said nothing.

"Do you mind if we take a walk around your home and see what's going on?" Alex asked.

"By all means," Patsy replied.

Instantly and in unison, the boys piped up, "Can we come too?"

Alex looked at Zoey and she saw the concern in his eyes. This was all new to them; they didn't know what they'd find. Nor did they know if the children's strong emotional energies would cloud the team's sensitivities. Yet, at the same time, knowing part of what the group needed to learn was detachment in all senses, Alex figured this was a good opportunity to practice being present. With a nod of his head, he agreed they could tag along.

The group moved out into the home. Zoey and Nell went upstairs while Ariel, Alex, and the boys explored the downstairs. Each group took photographs and conducted EVP sessions. Then they reversed location, with Zoey and Nell taking the downstairs while Ariel, Alex, and the children wandered through the two bedrooms. No one in the group could shake the anxiety dogging their heels, yet they kept to the task at hand.

Alex, in particular, felt as though someone was following him as he moved through the upstairs. The energy was heavy, filled with the apprehension they were all feeling. To his relief, it lacked menace. Although he'd lived his life relying on his instincts, this ghost-hunting business was still new to all of them. Better to get their feet wet with a benign haunting than to deal with something darker right out of the gate.

He noticed, however, the children were edgy and sticking closer to him.

When he entered the master bedroom, he lifted his camera to take pictures. Throughout the lens, he saw what appeared to be a shadow person standing next to the bed where, going by the articles on the night stand, Patsy slept. He slowly lowered the camera and was astonished to see the full apparition of a man come into focus. Beside him, Ariel caught her breath. The boys grabbed her as though something had spooked them.

"What is it?" Ariel asked them.

"We're feeling the creepies," the older boy responded.

"The creepies?"

"Yeah. It's like what we feel at night."

Alex studied the spirit. He was dressed in jeans and a denim shirt. He bore a strong resemblance to Patsy. The energy emanating from him was one of sadness and guilt, along with an anxiety that felt almost static. In his mind, Alex heard the word "senseless" repeated over and over again. Suddenly, he experienced a sharp pain behind his eyes. He automatically closed them as he took a step back. When he reopened his eyes, the spirit was gone.

"Oh my goodness," was all Ariel could say as they looked to the now-empty space near the bed.

"It feels funny in here," the youngest boy piped up. "Are we going to be okay?"

Alex felt the fear from the children. He adjusted his energy to fill them with calm and said, "Yes. We will make sense of this."

Downstairs, Zoey stood in the center of the living room. She was getting ready to do an EVP session when she heard the distinct roar of a motorcycle. She looked out the window, but the street was quiet. Wondering if she'd imagined it, she turned away from the curtains, only to hear it again. It took her a moment to realize she wasn't hearing the sounds from outside the house. She was hearing the roar of the motorcycle within her own head. Guessing this was a clue to the spirit who was haunting the house, she filed it away in the back of her mind and rejoined the others, who had by now gathered in the kitchen.

"So what's happening here?" Brian asked.

"There's definitely something going on in your home."

Before Alex could go on, he felt almost a physical pull towards the refrigerator. Taking a step towards it, he saw a collection of family photographs plastered all over one of the doors. He quietly scanned them. Suddenly he felt a sharp rush of energy envelope his body as he focused on one photograph in particular. It showed a much younger Patsy standing between two men. They had their arms around each other and were smiling broadly into the camera. Alex's eyes widened when he realized the taller of the men was the same man he'd seen upstairs in the master bedroom. He felt the hairs on the back of his neck stand on end and knew the spirit had walked up behind him.

"He's pointing to this photograph," Alex announced.

Patsy drew near. "That was taken about ten years ago. The guy on the right is my younger brother Paulie. The other was my older brother Mitch."

Ariel swallowed a gasp. That was the name she'd heard in the car on the way over. Once again the group felt a rush of tingles at the mention of the name.

"What did I just feel?" Patsy exclaimed. "My whole body is covered in goose bumps." They all felt her fear. Once again, Alex tried to reassure her. "Don't worry, Patsy. We're getting closer to an answer. Just hang in there."

She took a deep breath and nodded.

"I heard the sound of a motorcycle when I was in the living room earlier," Zoey replied. "And we've all been suffering from headaches since we arrived."

Patsy sucked in her breath. "I've been getting headaches for a few months now. I've been to the doctors but they can't figure out what they are."

As Patsy spoke, the feelings of anxiety spiked up again.

"You guys feeling this?" Alex asked.

"The creepies!" the boys yelled out.

"It's okay, boys," Alex replied. He settled into an open, calming energy, which immediately had an effect on the children.

"What are the creepies?" Nell asked.

"You know," the oldest answered. "Cold tingles."

"Does it frighten you when you feel the creepies?"

They both nodded. "Kinda. We feel the creepies, then we wake up and see a man standing at the foot of our beds."

"They see him almost every night," Patsy replied. "It's getting to a point where they're afraid to go to bed."

"We've been experiencing these weird feelings," Brian admitted. "It started a few months ago, right around the same time Patsy started getting her headaches and the boys started seeing the man in their room. It's like we want to jump out of our skins, but we don't know why. I guess it's like the creepies the boys are talking about."

"He's not here to hurt you. He's extremely anxious and afraid. He feels he has to give you something—some kind of message," Alex said.

"Who is he anyway?"

Alex took his time answering. He needed to make sure he was truly feeling the energy of the moment and not the feelings of the family or his own feelings of what was going on. He found himself letting go more. He erased all judgment, all fear. He made no projections of his own experience that could cloud the moment. In that instant, he began to feel all of what the spirit was about.

He pointed to the photograph on the fridge, resting his finger on the image of Mitch. "When I was upstairs in the master bedroom, I saw him standing by your side of the bed, Patsy."

Patsy visibly reacted. She unconsciously leaned against her husband for support. "He—he died in a motorcycle accident five years ago," she whispered.

Once again the group felt a sharp shift in energy, as if Mitch was letting them know that they were indeed feeling his presence. By staying open, a rush of information flooded Alex's mind.

"Mitch wasn't a very nice person, was he?" Alex asked gently.

Patsy's eyes watered as she shook her head. "He got mixed up with the wrong people. He started dealing drugs. He used to be so sweet when he was a kid. But then, when he got older . . . well, he had a temper that he found hard to control sometimes."

"I keep hearing the word 'senseless.' He feels his death was senseless."

Patsy nodded. "It pretty much was. He'd been out drinking with his buddies after work. He knew he was drunk; in fact, a couple of his friends tried to stop him from getting on his bike. But Mitch could never show weakness. Even if he was plastered, which he was, he'd never show it. So he climbed on his bike and ended up missing a curve in the road. He hit a telephone pole."

The group held steady as a series of strong emotions ran through them. Simultaneously, they felt guilt, regret, and the acute anxiety.

"Did Mitch die from massive head trauma?" Alex asked. Patsy nodded. Then, as if the pieces started to fall into place, she looked up sharply at Alex.

"Are those the headaches I've been getting?"

"Yes. He's still holding onto the physical pain he suffered, even though he's no longer in a body."

Zoey took a step forward. "He's very sorry for the way he treated you and his family, Patsy. He realizes now what a jerk he was. He's trying to make up for it by warning you about Paulie."

"Paulie?"

"Yes. He doesn't want Paulie to go down the same road he did."

Patsy put her hand to her mouth and closed her eyes against the welling tears. "We think Paulie is starting to get involved with drugs."

"And he just started riding a motorcycle a few months ago," Brian added.

The energy spiked again. "What did I just feel?" Patsy gasped.

"That was Mitch reacting to Brian's words," Alex explained. "He's here to warn you to keep an eye on Paulie. As Zoey said, he doesn't want Paulie to end up the way he did."

"Is there anything we can do to help him get to—well—wherever spirits go when they die?" Brian asked as he slipped a reassuring arm around Patsy's shoulders. "I don't want him to be stuck here, afraid and sorry and guilty. It's not fair. I'm sure if he knew what awaited him, he would have changed."

The group looked at each other. They all felt they wanted to help Mitch.

But how?

"Why don't we try to change the energy? Let's all get into a circle and hold hands, including the boys," Alex offered. "By combining our energies, we may be able to do something for Mitch. Notice how each time we felt the tingles, we felt him connect his energy with us." The group formed a circle in the middle of the small kitchen. "Now close your eyes."

Alex felt the tingles getting stronger and stronger within him, as if Mitch was sensing the love everyone in the circle had for him. At the same time, he felt a higher frequency come in—his energetic vibration increasing exponentially. He realized in that moment that as he gathered people together with the intention of changing the energy, a higher vibration flowed within him. Opening his eyes, he saw it in the others as well. It was as though this energy was beginning to make him feel lighter, more alive, as if the very air around them was dancing. He also noticed that as the higher vibration of energy came in, Mitch was becoming more present. Words appeared in his mind and he began to speak.

"We stand here before you, as your family, as your friends. For those who knew you, they knew the choices you made in life were not always the best choices. But in death, you now have an opportunity to be forgiven by the living. We ask in this moment that you let go of all the guilt and shame and worry that you believe you created in life. In this moment, we are a light. We are love. We recognize that no one is left behind. Everyone who asks can be forgiven. In this moment, we are the light of that forgiveness. May you feel now that which you chased but could not touch in life. May you feel now the love and peace you never knew in life. Know there is now an open door. Through that door is an open heart that sees you as perfect."

As Alex spoke, he felt Mitch's regrets over the life he'd led begin to change. His vibration increased and the area where he stood was now filled with a luminescent light.

The group felt a tingling go through them, starting at their feet and rising up through the tops of their heads.

Alex gave a little shudder. Then opened his eyes. He saw tears streaming down Patsy's face.

"I feel goosebumps all over me," Patsy said through her tears. "Especially my feet. What is that?"

"I believe you're grounding out the heavier energy of what Mitch was in life," Alex answered.

Patsy's face was in awe. "I felt as though he walked through me. I'm not quite sure if I can explain it, but it was as if Mitch's soul kissed my soul. As if he hugged me as he left. It was—" she filled up with tears again. "It was beautiful."

"Mommy, Mommy, the creepies are gone!" the boys shouted out.

"Yes," Patsy responded. "The creepies are gone."

Afterwards, in the car ride home, Alex talked about what had just happened.

"I'm proud of all of you," he began. "You didn't get caught up in the drama energy. You were able to keep everything and everyone calm. You focused on the energy. Because of that, you were able to connect with Mitch and see why he was there. We allowed whatever needed to unfold to do so. It's as if each of you turned a light on in your hearts. By not judging, by staying open, it allowed Mitch to use us to ground out the heavy energy of what was keeping him here. He was then able to use our higher vibrational energy to move on." He turned to look at Nell. "Do you remember asking what the point of all this is? Why we feel what we feel? Here is your answer. We feel what we feel because we have the ability to help a spirit get home."

"Wow," Nell said. "Now that I understand, I can't think of a greater gift to give a wandering spirit."

CHANGING THE ENERGY

We have perceptions of the afterlife that may be just theories or guesswork. Yet, as an empath, these theories and guesswork are put to the test. As we have discovered in our lives as empaths, we feel continuously. But once in a while, we get a feeling that cannot be understood. Where are these feelings coming from? Where are those random thoughts and mysterious tingles coming from? They are all bits and pieces of a puzzle that can be crafted into some kind of knowing of what is happening in a particular space at a particular moment. So it was with this investigation and all the investigations we've done. We go into them as open as we can, with an understanding that everything is energy, whether it's coming from the living or the dead. Our only job is to be able to discern which is which. Once we discern, we practice the ability of understanding why the haunting is taking place in the first place. If it's true that everything is energy, then that energy needs a place to ground. It needs a force to feed it. Energy needs something to perpetuate it. Is it the space feeding the energy? The living? Is it the need of the dead to give a message? A warning? Or to simply feed off the drama and emotions of the living. All of these are energy thought processes that keep something here. But in our ability as empaths or as someone who can change the energetic frequency, is it possible that we can complete that drama or cycle of needing to help with the realization that help may be as simple as sensing the energy that you believe to be missing? Compassion to a wandering spirit? Forgiveness to a spirit in distress?

One of the questions we're asked has to do with our decision, at the outset of forming our paranormal investigative team, to help the dead cross. Many people feel we are usurping the position of a supreme being by assisting the dead. What we've discovered is that, just as we have free will in life, we also have it in death. We cannot force a spirit to leave if they don't want to leave. However, we've found that in countless instances, the spirits don't know they have a choice. They are stuck in a space between this earthly plane and the next. What we, and countless other people like us who are taking their investigations that one step further, do is offer the spirit a choice by using our energies to help them release those emotions that are keeping them bound in the first place. Once they realize they can move on, many choose to do so.

Although realizing one of the purposes of their empathy was the ability to help spirits move on, there were other important lessons to learn.

One of the more important ones had to do with discernment.

Having heard the name "Mitch" before their investigation, Ariel realized she had the ability to communicate with the dead. Fired up, she was determined to learn all she could about the gift of mediumship.

She'd heard through a girlfriend that a well-known local psychic was coming to her home to give what she called "Messages from Above." The psychic claimed she had the ability to connect with loved ones and give whatever messages the dead wanted to give to the living. Because she'd come so highly recommended, Ariel took a chance and immediately reserved spots for herself and her friends to see the psychic and discover what this message giving was all about. A week later found the four of them, along with three other women, seated in the living room of her friend's spacious suburban home.

"She's supposed to be one of the best," Ariel whispered to her friends. "I can't wait for this to begin. Maybe she can explain these voices we hear in our heads!"

A few minutes later, a middle-aged woman came out of the bedroom and stood in front of the couch and chairs where the group was seated. She was dressed in a stylish print dress, with a scarf smartly wrapped around her throat and her grey hair cut in a chic bob. Her rich perfume wafted throughout the living room.

"I'm so happy you could come tonight," she said in a pleasant voice. "My name is Connie Collier. I've been a medium for more than thirty years, helping relatives connect with their departed loved ones. I've already prepared the room tonight to receive those who wish to communicate with you. It may be loved ones, old friends, guides, angels, anyone who has a message they wish to share. So, let's get started. I feel the gathering of spirits who are most eager to speak!"

Zoey and Alex glanced at each other. They weren't feeling anything except the anticipation of the women.

Connie scanned the group carefully, her eyes bouncing back and forth. Her gaze eventually settled on Nell and she pointed a long finger at the nurse.

"I see a man with you," she said to Nell. "He is of medium height, with dark hair and a moustache. He appears to be in his mid-fifties."

Nell appeared astonished and gave a slight nod of her head. Alex suddenly felt Nell's energy opening up in response to the possibility of having such a connection made. Nell's walls came down and her energy expanded like an open book.

Connie continued. "He feels like a brother. Does that make sense to you?"

Nell gave a small start. "Yes," she replied.

Connie's demeanor changed. The connection was complete. "He says you were always his favorite sister. He's sending you much love from the Other Side. Oh, he loved to wear bow-ties, didn't he? He had quite a collection of them."

Zoey and Alex once again glanced at each other. They didn't want to admit it, but they still weren't feeling anything except Nell's energy, which changed once she heard Connie's last statement. The startlement Nell had initially felt was now gone and her walls began to close again.

For a moment Zoey wondered if maybe they were losing the abilities their empathic gifts gave them of communicating with the Other Side. There weren't the tingles she and Alex usually felt when spirits were near. Nor were they seeing any shadow people.

Just who was this medium communicating with?

She glanced around the room, trying to make sure she wasn't missing any shadow people that might be lurking. Seeing nothing, she turned back to Connie. As she did so, she swallowed a gasp. Instead of seeing spirits, she instead saw what appeared to be a light colored cord snaking its way from Connie's belly to Nell's belly. She'd never seen anything like that before and didn't know what to think. She nudged Alex. He nodded. He'd seen it, too.

They looked to the other participants. Were they the only ones seeing this cord? Apparently so, because the women were enraptured by Connie's message to Nell. The two friends watched in complete amazement as Nell's reading came to an end. As Connie finished, the cord detached from Nell and seemed to be searching a new place of attachment for the next reading.

Connie was getting closer to Zoey and Alex. The two glanced at each other. With a smile, Zoey leaned in to Alex and whispered, "What do you think? Do you want to be speared with that cord we're seeing?"

"Let's open up more and see what happens."

The two companions opened their hearts and minds. They let go of any preconceived notions or judgments of what was going on there that night. Instead, they felt their energetic vibrations increase until it seemed to fill the room. No thoughts. No projections. Just energy.

Connie turned to them and they immediately noticed her discomfort. She seemed startled, as if she was trying to search for something but couldn't find it. Finally, she just shook her head. "You two must be close because the energy from both of you is very strong. I'm sorry, but I'm not getting anything for you. I guess no one from beyond wishes to give you a message," she exclaimed with an embarrassed laugh before quickly turning to the next woman to get a reading.

As soon as they got in the car to go home, Ariel sighed.

"Wasn't she awesome? I can't believe she picked up on my mediumship abilities. It was exactly what I needed to hear!"

"She was awful!" Nell declared.

Ariel was surprised. "Why do you say that?"

"Because first of all, my brother was a complete loser. He didn't love anyone but himself. I wanted to love him, but he made it so hard. He completely ignored me. That is, unless he wanted money. Then he'd basically make my life a living hell until I gave him what he wanted. To be honest, I was worried this mediumship stuff was real and that he might show up. I was thinking about him the whole way here."

Ariel turned to Zoey and Alex. "I wonder why you two didn't get any messages."

"I'm not sure," Alex admitted. "We were about as open as can be. At that moment I felt I had nothing to hide. I was just beaming like a bright light bulb. Maybe we made it harder for her to read for us, but in a way that proves a point. Is a medium supposed to be accessing our energy or the energy of a spirit? When you think about it, we made it easier for her to connect to a spirit. We had no clouded judgment or thoughts projecting from us. Isn't that what really is supposed to happen?"

The woman frowned. "You're not making any sense."

Alex shifted in his seat so he could look directly at Ariel. "My guess is that since we've been working on ourselves and doing our best to heal our issues, our energy is higher in vibration. I don't believe Connie is accustomed to that high vibrational energy. She was overwhelmed by it. When we do our circles during investigations, we need to settle into that high energy that comes in. Never having encountered it before, she probably couldn't settle in. She didn't know what to do. So she just moved on."

Zoey nodded. "We didn't see or feel any spirits in that room. What we did see was a cord that stretched from Connie to whoever she was giving a message to. As soon as she finished with that person, the cord detached and reattached itself to the next person she read for."

"Wait a minute. Are you telling me she had a cord into *me* when she gave me that bogus message?" Nell demanded.

"I'm afraid so. And it really wasn't a bogus message, if you think about it. It was just Connie's interpretation of what she was seeing."

Ariel turned to Alex. "What do you think that cord was?" she asked him.

"I hate to say this, but I think that's how she was getting her information."

"Huh?"

"Have you heard of the aura?" Nell and Ariel shook their heads. "The aura is basically an energy container that surrounds every human being. It holds information about our past, our present, and our future, including memories of the people in your life. That's why some psychics are good at predicting what's going to happen to a person, where they've come from, and what's going on presently in their lives. It also is what allows them to describe relatives, loved ones, people you know. It's all there catalogued in your aura. Who's to say that Connie, as a medium, wasn't reading *your* energy instead of actually communicating with your brother, who, by the way, none of us felt was even in that room. Ariel, maybe she was reading in your aura, your need to find out more about your mediumship abilities."

"Wow, would Connie deliberately do that?"

"To be honest, I don't believe she's even aware of it. We've all felt the presence of spirits with us. We've felt that familiar tingle in the back of our heads and shoulders, or the cold drop in temperature when a spirit of a lower vibration comes into our space. None of that was there tonight. Yet Connie was getting her information from somewhere. Since she doesn't seem to understand how energy works, she believed she was speaking to a spirit, when in actuality, what she was really doing was simply reading your energy and interpreting it in a positive way. No one would go for a reading if it was all bad news. True?" They all nodded. "Nell, you said you were thinking about him on the way to the reading, fearful and worried that he might show up. If you think about it, that's a pretty strong energy you were projecting. I bet all those feelings were attached to a strong memory of what he looked like."

"You're right. I was picturing him as we drove here. I remembered his favorite suit and—" she paused for a moment before continuing, "and his huge collection of bow-ties."

"I believe all of that was transmitted to Connie through that cord we saw. You actually made it easy for her when you suddenly opened up at the beginning of her reading for you. I'm guessing she was simply seeing your thoughts and memories of your brother and interpreting them as something positive without acknowledging the emotional pain you experienced with him."

"If that could happen to an experienced medium like Connie, it could happen to anyone," Zoey replied.

"It seems to me that the only way to discern whether you're really talking to a spirit is to feel their energy around you. We all felt Mitch's energy. We felt Mr. Astoria's energy when we went to the séance. Which brings up something else I've been thinking about."

"This should be interesting," Zoey joked.

"It is. Just about everyone tonight received the same message. Someone from the other side loves you. They're looking after you. Or they're sorry for something they did to hurt you. One of the ladies was told her grandmother loved her pearls, while another was told her grandfather's favorite color was blue. Although those messages may be nice to hear, at the end of the day, what purpose do they serve?"

"What do you mean?"

"I'm beginning to see that this gift of mediumship needs to come from an open heart. In other words, true mediumship is helping people on their path, helping them let go of things that hinder them from living a more fulfilling life. Maybe it's also about helping the spirits who are stuck. How is being told your grandmother loved her pearls or your grandfather's favorite color was blue fulfilling that? True healing happens when the love within one's open heart is so deep it doesn't need to be painted as rainbows and unicorns. It is harder to see the failures of true human experience. Everyone wants to hide their dark side. But isn't unconditional love what we're striving for?"

"Before tonight, I would have thought that kind of evidence was proof the medium was speaking to a spirit," Nell said. "But now that I know about this cord, I'd have to question that. And you're right about the quality of the message. Knowing my brother loved his bow-ties doesn't help me get on with my life or learn whatever lessons I'm meant to learn. It doesn't help me release my anger towards him. It actually makes it worse. I mean, really? I was his favorite sister?"

Alex looked to each of the women. "I think we're on to something here."

THE GIFT OF
MEDIUMSHIP

As an empath, our life is spent trying to understand why we feel what we do, where the feelings come from, and what they mean to us. Most empaths believe that feeling the energy is the only experience that defines them as an empath. If we pay attention, we eventually come to the conclusion that no matter what we feel, it's all just energy.

With further openness to our experience of energy, it begins to expand into other gifts, including the gifts of the four "clairs": clairaudiance, the ability to hear spirit; clairvoyance, the ability to see spirit; claircognizance, the ability to know the truth about something; clairsentience, the ability to feel emotion from a spirit. Yet each of these clairs is simply an experience of understanding and reading energy, something that an empath learns very quickly. Out of this, another gift is mediumship, the ability to communicate with spirit.

As an empath, you not only feel and understand the emotional complexity of the living, but you can grasp the same from the dead. For this reason, many empaths attract more spirits to themselves. Some spirits feel cold, some feel warm, some feel sad, some feel angry. This isn't a bad thing if you begin to see these experiences as teaching you where a spirit is energetically in that moment. It's the same opportunity for those who do readings. The discernment is in knowing where the information is coming from. Are you actually feeling the presence of a spirit, or are you reading a living person's auric field? There is a difference. As we discussed in earlier chapters, there is something called place memory—an energy that is burned into time. Is it possible that a memory can be burned into the living's auric field through trauma? We say yes. We feel that as empaths, by feeling from the living, we can begin to understand why they're sad or in pain or angry. It's also easy to see how these energies can keep a person stuck in their lives.

But can it also keep us stuck in the afterlife? Carrying the judgments in life that have created a less than ideal emotional experience? As empaths, we feel the dead's anger, sadness, grief, attachments, etc. This is where the quality of a reading received from a medium can be important. We have met many mediums who, like Connie, are not really communicating with the dead, but reading a client's auric field. They're not being dishonest—they simply don't know that is what they're doing. We're not trying to beat up on mediums. We know many mediums who do communicate with Spirit. The point we're trying to make here is that discernment allows you to make better choices with the information you're receiving or giving.

Getting a message that your grandmother liked to garden may be all well and good. This may even give you confirmation that she is present and all is well. But is this true? Is it possible that you miss your grandmother so much you often think of her gardening? Is it possible when you walked in for your reading that you were thinking about your grandmother; how much you loved and missed her? Can that be what the medium is reading? Does this assist you in having an understanding of the afterlife?

What if, instead, you felt a physical presence walk into the room that can't be seen, but is felt? You'd know a presence is there because your hair stands on end. You feel the back of your neck or head tingle. Or perhaps feel a very strong emotional presence. Rather than become afraid, you choose to experience the energy of the moment without reacting from your own judgement or preconceived ideas of what this energy needs to be. Suddenly you feel sad. You sit in this sadness, seeing it only as the truth of what you're experiencing in that moment. As you allow this, the sadness begins to explain itself by words, mental images, a knowing, even a conversation of something that may have been missed or desired in life that was unfulfilled. As the reading continues, you begin to realize how human this spirit is. The more they release energetically, the more the room begins to change and lighten up. More information flows in. We say this is a gift. It's nice that your grandmother liked to garden, but would you rather know who your grandmother really was in life? Herein lies the lesson of discernment.

As an empath, you are an expert in feeling energy. The next step is learning the valuable lesson of discernment. Discerning what you feel and where that energy is coming from allows you to navigate the world of mediumship. Energy from an evolved spirit will definitely get your attention. The vibration is much higher—it's as though your entire body is vibrating. Information from an evolved spirit is worth considering. They know your life, the lessons you're here to learn. They know they can't interfere with your free will because they have evolved to a place of unconditional love—a vibration the living all strive to attain. It's not that the lesser vibrations do not teach or are not helpful. They also can show you the responsibilities and the consequences of choices made in life.

Therefore, is it wrong for a medium to read your auric field rather than communicate directly with spirit, even if they believe they are? Not totally. If it brings you comfort, eases your grief, and allows you to release your memories in that moment, how can that be wrong?

However, what if there is more to what we are experiencing as empaths? What if in what we feel from those in the afterlife, which isn't always warm and fuzzy, we can help them finish their journey? Think about those instances when, as an empath, you've felt a friend in distress, only to be told that they're fine. You know they're not. You can physically feel they're upset. By being the sensitive friend, you can eventually allow them to open up and release what is distressing them. If a medium is reading your auric field instead of communicating with an actual spirit, or who insists on only giving information that is rainbows and unicorns, is that denying a ghost in distress from releasing that which holds them here?

Does that deny us the ability to learn from the dead? Can we begin to understand the importance and responsibilities of all our living connections and energetic choices before we find ourselves on the Other Side?

INTERACTION

Alex and his team continued to do small investigations, adding to the body of knowledge they were acquiring about the Other Side and how their empathic gifts impacted that knowledge. Using what they'd learned after their experience with the spirit of Mitch, they began to help whatever spirits they encountered to move on.

Unknown to them, they were garnering a reputation throughout the paranormal investigative community regarding this ability. There weren't many teams that actually removed a ghost from a haunted site. Alex and his group learned it took more than waving sage and using crystals to help a spirit move on. It had to do with energy and their growing ability to raise their vibrations high enough to help the ghost shed whatever earthbound emotions they were still holding onto. By doing this, their combined light allowed the ghost to realize they had a choice to stay or move on. Many chose to move on.

It wasn't long before they were invited to participate in a joint investigation with another local paranormal investigation team.

"I want to see how you guys work," Boris, the leader of Ghostly Paranormal Team or GPT said when he called up Alex one evening. "There's a bar in Boston we've been called on to check out. It was only built a few months ago, but the owner is saying all kinds of things are going on. I thought our two teams could work together on this. He's closing Thursday night at eleven, so we'll need to do our thing after that."

Alex agreed, and that Thursday the two teams rode together in the GPT's van towards The Gray Goose, the bar they were set to investigate.

The GPT team was made up of Boris, his girlfriend, Maddie, and Boris' brother, Jerry, who manned the monitors they set up. As Boris explained to Alex and his team as he drove down the highway towards their destination, they'd gotten involved in ghost investigations because of their own experiences.

"Jerry and I grew up in a haunted house," the thirty-five-year-old leader shared with Alex, Zoey, Nell, and Ariel. "It was an old farmhouse, probably about seventy-five years old when we moved in. We were always seeing shadow people ducking around corners. My mom and dad constantly had their things moved around. They blamed us, but we knew it was the spirits that lived in the house with us."

"I take it your parents didn't think you had ghosts," Zoey asked.

"Hell no. That was something they wouldn't wrap their minds around. But I have a feeling they knew *something* was going on. They just wouldn't admit it to us. We finally moved out when I was ten and Jerry was eight."

"What about you, Maddie?" Nell asked. "Did you have ghostly encounters growing up as well?"

The tall, statuesque redhead shook her head. "It wasn't so much that I saw stuff. I grew up extremely sensitive. I knew when someone was having a bad day even if they didn't say anything. And sometimes I'd know when something was going to happen before it did. That used to completely freak me out."

"It seems to me all of you are empaths just as we are," Alex said.

The three nodded. "We've been told that," Boris said.

It was close to eleven-thirty in the evening when the van finally pulled to a stop before a tavern located on a strip of land that jutted out into Boston Harbor. There was a sign with a grey goose hanging outside, swinging in the brisk breeze that came up off the water. Piling out of the van, Alex's group stood outside and looked up at the sign, soaking in the energies that surrounded them.

"What a beautiful spot," Zoey remarked as she took in the colorful night lights of Boston across the harbor from where the bar was located.

"The energy actually doesn't feel that bad," Ariel concluded.

"You're right. We'll see how it feels inside," Alex replied.

Boris knocked on the large wooden door and they were swiftly let in. Inside the lighting was low, but the ambiance was very welcoming. There was a long bar that took up one side of the room. A large ornate mirror hung on the wall behind the bar, below which stood a wide collection of neatly stacked liquor bottles. On the other side of the room were tables and chairs where the patrons would eat and drink. On the far side was a small stage where local bands played on the weekends.

A man locked the door behind them. He was in his fifties, with salt-and-pepper hair and goatee. He was a bit heavyset and stern-looking, yet when he smiled, it illuminated his face.

"My name is Sean," he said in a thick Boston accent as he shook everyone's hands. "I'm the owner. Glad you guys could make it."

"So what's been happening here?" Boris asked.

Sean absently scratched the back of his head, his features looking a bit sheepish. "I gotta tell you, I never believed in any of this ghost stuff. I always thought it was a bunch of hooey. But ever since I opened up a few months ago, there's been things happening here that I can't explain. And believe me, I've tried." He turned and pointed to the bar. "Down at the end of the bar, I've had glasses move on their own. I've seen it happen several times. Two weeks ago, I lost a manager who says she saw the image of a man in that mirror one night when she was closing up. Scared the bejesus out of her so much she quit right then and there. The weird thing is that this place is new. It used to be an empty lot before we bought it and built this place."

"Have you physically felt anything yourself?" Alex asked.

"Once in a while, especially when I'm cleaning up at night, I'll walk around and suddenly feel as though I've walked through a curtain. It's hard to explain, but when I do that, I get the shivers. My hair stands on end. Then just as quickly as it happens, it goes away." He paused, then frowned. "Now that I think about it, when that's happened to me, I've gotten the strongest sensation that I'm being watched."

Alex's group exchanged glances. Even though one of their rules was not to ask particulars so they could keep the energy clear, they sensed it was okay. Something was different there.

As Sean continued his story, Zoey quietly detached herself and wandered over to the end of the bar where the glasses were supposed to have moved. With her senses alert, she tried to feel the presence of any spirits that might be lurking about. She'd learned to know when a spirit was present by the tingles she'd feel on her shoulders or on the back of her head. She also knew the signs of a spirit being present when she'd suddenly feel a pressure in her chest or a tightness in her belly.

Standing at the end of the bar, Zoey abruptly felt dizzy. The room spun and it took all her effort not to fall down. Rather than panic, she slowly ground out the energy and was soon able to loosen the grip the energy had on her. She said nothing as she walked back towards the groups.

"Okay, let's set up our equipment and see what we get," Boris announced.

With an expertise borne of their many investigations, the GPT team soon had cameras and monitors going. Meanwhile, Alex and his team wandered about, relying on their empathic abilities to tell them what was going on at The Grey Goose.

The room was large enough that both teams didn't step on each other's toes. EVP sessions were recorded, photos were taken, and Alex and his friends stepped back to allow Boris and his team to conduct their by-the-book investigation.

Zoey pulled Alex aside and told him what she'd experienced at the bar. Alex nodded and unobtrusively went to stand where she'd stood. He closed his eyes and opened his mind. It wasn't long before he too felt the dizziness. He made a mental note of what he was seeing and feeling, then quietly asked Ariel and Nell to stand at the bar. He wasn't surprised when they reported feeling the same dizziness as he and Zoey.

Finally, after a couple of hours, Boris felt they had enough information to call it a night. They'd been able to capture a few orbs flying about the tavern and Maddie had gotten an EVP of a ghostly voice whispering the word, "drink". They were excited over their findings and couldn't wait to review more of the tapes when they got home.

"How would you folks like a beer before you go? It's on the house as a way of saying thank you for coming out here tonight," Sean announced.

Boris nodded. "Great! Thanks!" He stood near the end of the bar where Alex and his group had their experience. Alex and his team watched carefully as Boris knocked back a beer. However, instead of stopping, he asked for another. Standing next to Maddie, Alex overheard her whisper to Jerry, "What's up with Boris? He never drinks like that."

Jerry shrugged. "I don't know, but I'd better stop him if he's driving us home tonight."

Alex and his group exchanged glances. They knew exactly what was going on. A silent agreement passed between all of them. Alex turned to Jerry.

"Your brother has a spirit standing behind him. I think that's why he's drinking the way he is."

Jerry looked at Alex incredulously.

"When any of your team stood where he's standing, did you get dizzy?" Zoey asked.

"As a matter of fact, now that you mention it, I did get dizzy there," Maddie responded.

"I did too," Jerry admitted.

Alex turned to Sean. "Have you ever heard of the concept 'like energy attracts like energy'?"

"Not really."

"We've discovered that when a person dies, if he's holding on to any earth bound emotion, he seeks out that emotion of the living. In other words, because this is a bar, you're attracting the ghosts of people who were alcoholics in life because that's the energy they're accustomed to feeling. Because Boris is so sensitive, he doesn't realize that the need to drink he's feeling isn't coming from him. It's coming from the spirit standing behind him. The same goes for the dizziness we all felt standing where he's standing. I'm pretty sure that dizziness isn't so much dizziness as the feeling you get when you've had a bit too much to drink."

"You're right," Maddie said. "I felt more buzzed than anything else."

Sean frowned. "So you're telling me that ghost was here even before we built the place?"

"Not necessarily. It doesn't matter how old a place is. This building could be a week old and you'd still get a haunting. It all has to do with that theory I mentioned—like energy attracting like energy. In your case, a man who died an alcoholic is wandering about, seeking the energy of a living person who likes to drink. He's standing so close to Boris that his energy is intermingling with Boris'. That's why Boris wants to keep drinking. It's not really him, but the ghost standing behind him."

"I'm also getting a sense that the ghost was a bit of a character in life," Nell replied. "It doesn't matter that's he no longer living. His personality traits have stayed with him. He's the one moving your glasses about. He's also the one who appeared to your manager in the mirror. He fed off the energy of the reaction your manager had when she saw him. He also feeds off the reaction of anyone who sees the glasses move."

"That curtain you described when you walk around here is you literally walking through him," Zoey continued.

"Jeez . . ." Sean muttered as he fell back into one of the chairs.

"One of the biggest things we've discovered in our investigations is that drama in life equals drama in death. Until your ghostly friend moves on, he'll continue to play pranks and jokes just as he did in life."

"What can we do to get him to leave?" Sean asked.

"We show him he has a choice. Right now, he doesn't have a clue that he can leave this place. He's still too bound by earthly ties to see the doorway into a better place."

"How do we do that?"

"By using our energy. Let's all gather in a circle."

They pulled Boris away from the bar and the two groups, including Sean, got into a large circle. They held hands and once again Alex spoke about forgiveness, about not judging the spirit.

"You no longer need to hold on to what you were in life," Alex said. "You have the ability to go to that place of profound peace and love. Let go of all that binds you here and use our light and energy to light your way forward. That which alcohol gives you does not compare to where you are going."

Each of the members of GPT felt themselves covered in goose bumps as their vibrations increased. Even Sean felt a bit lightheaded as their combined energies brought the vibration higher.

"My feet are tingling," Sean exclaimed.

"You're helping to ground out all the earthly emotions and the energy of alcohol from your ghostly friend," Alex explained.

The bar filled with an emotion of such unconditional love that it almost brought the GPT team to their knees. It felt as though the very top of their heads were opening up. A whoosh of energy filled the room. Then it was over.

"He's gone," Alex announced.

Boris shook his head as Maddie and Jerry walked around the bar. "It feels different in here," she said.

"Yeah. It's much lighter," Jerry concurred.

Boris looked to Alex and smiled. "Brother, you have to teach me how to do that. It's more than just proving or disproving the existence of a ghost, isn't it? The ability to help a spirit actually move on to a better place will give meaning to why we do what we do."

Alex returned his smile. "Exactly."

THE TIES THAT
BIND

As people go about trying to prove or disprove the existence of ghosts, as an empath you don't need to prove anything. You experience things so deeply on such a soul level, whether it's seeing shadow people, or having unexplained experiences of dread or pain. We've been amazed that in many of the investigations we've been to, where the majority of participants are sensitive, we've had much more paranormal interaction. It's as though we attract them—not in a bad way, but in the way that we are a light to them. When you are dealing with a lost soul, they will invariably be attracted to a light. This light could be what helps them. You, as an empath, are that light. By the same token, we've discovered there are many things in our lives that bind us in death to this earthly world. It could be holding on to anger or grief or thinking you've left something undone that you believe needs to be finished before you can move on. By holding on to these heavier emotions, it doesn't allow a spirit to pass on to a better place. Some of the harder ties that bind a spirit to the living are addiction. How many times have you walked into a room and smelled the smell of alcohol or smelled the unmistakable scent of cigarettes or cigar smoke? Is it possible these are spirits reaching out in their need to still feel the energy of alcohol and smoking? What happened at The Grey Goose in this story is not unusual. It happens more often than you might think. It's a perfect example of the ties that bind the dead to the living.

DEMON

I'VE GOT A DEMON IN MY HOUSE!

Summer was just around the corner

Summer was just around the corner. The group had now been doing investigations for almost six months. With each case, they were learning more and more about energy, especially in how the energy of the living was more closely tied to the energy of the dead than people realized.

Alex had just come home from work when his phone rang. He barely said hello before a hysterical caller screamed into his ear, "I've got a demon in my house! You have to help me!"

"Wh—what?" Alex stammered.

"My name is Rose. I heard you and your group get rid of spirits. I'm telling you, I HAVE A DEMON IN MY HOUSE!"

Alex froze. He had no experience with this. Did he really want to try and take on a demon? How would he even begin to try and deal with a demon? They didn't have enough knowledge between the four of them to deal with this situation. What if they made it worse?

"Give me your number. I'll talk to my team and get back to you."

He took her phone number and hung up before she could become hysterical again. His heart raced with fear as Rose's panicked energy ramped up his own feelings of dread. His first instinct was to refuse to investigate. Who in heaven's name would willingly investigate a demon?

Yet at the same time, he felt a bit disgusted with his cowardice. In the end, wasn't it all just energy? Yes, demonic energy might be darker, but if this case had been presented to them, perhaps it was presented because this was something they needed to do or learn.

He called up each of the ladies and asked if they wanted to look into it. There was hesitation and, like him, expressions of fear. Nell, in particular, was especially fearful.

"Do I need to go out and buy crucifixes and holy water?" she asked in all seriousness.

"I'm not sure how effective they'd be," Alex admitted. "They certainly don't seem to work on all the television shows we've watched."

"True. According to those shows, there are demons everywhere!" Nell exclaimed.

"If that's the case, it was inevitable we'd eventually run into one." He paused. "We've been safe so far. We cannot go into fear over this. From what I've seen, I guess demons thrive on fear. Everyone freaks out when they're mentioned, including us right now. So we'll go into this investigation with a sense of open caution."

A few days later, the group drove up the coast towards Portland, Maine. To their surprise, they didn't feel anything on the way, but decided not to jump to any conclusions because of it. It was always possible the demon was hiding and wouldn't make itself known until they arrived.

They finally pulled up to an old, ramshackle cottage near the ocean. They put out their energetic feelers to see if they could pick up on anything.

"The place is filled with history," Ariel replied as she walked around the front yard.

"Yet, there's something going on here," Alex said. "There's more than meets the eye. I feel an underlying—I don't know . . ."

Suddenly the front door was thrown open and a heavy, dark-haired woman wearing black leggings and an oversized T-shirt ran out. She was frantically waving her arms at them. "You're here to save me from the demon! Oh, thank God you're here."

The entire group took a collective step backwards as they were besieged by her feelings of abject fear, angst, and a host of other emotions they couldn't even begin to decipher.

"We'll try our best to help," Alex finally said.

"What are you going to do?"

"First, we need to figure what exactly is going on."

"I told you what's going on!" Rose shouted, once more on the brink of hysteria. "There's a damned demon in my house!"

Alex turned to the group. "Why don't you go inside and see what you feel. I'm going to stay out here and calm Rose down or else we'll never figure anything out. I need to break one of our rules and get to the bottom of who she is."

Zoey looked at him, her eyes filled with worry. Out of Rose's earshot, she asked, "Do you think she's crazy?"

"I'm not sure yet."

With a heavy heart, Zoey pulled Nell and Ariel along with her as they entered Rose's house. If Rose was crazy, she was apprehensive about leaving Alex alone with her.

Alex sat outside with Rose at an old picnic table. He began by asking questions about her life before gently working towards what made her believe she had a demon in her house. All the while, he couldn't let go of the feeling that she was holding something back. There was a secret she was unwilling to share with him. A strong, energetic instinct told him that whatever this secret was, it was the reason for the haunting.

"This thing keeps touching me and laughing at me and putting voices in my head. You've got to make it stop!"

Alex eyed her steadily. "There's something you're not telling me, Rose."

Her demeanor abruptly changed.

"That's not true," she said defiantly. However, he saw the fear in her eyes.

He stood up, knowing that if he continued pushing her, she'd completely shut down. "Let's go inside your house. The rest of the team may have something for us."

He met up with the ladies in the living room that was filled with so many knickknacks everyone was afraid to move lest they knock something over.

"What are you feeling?" he asked.

"It feels a lot like the energy we felt at The Grey Goose," Zoey said. "We actually talked about how each of us is dying for a drink, no pun intended."

Alex turned to Rose. "Do you like to drink?" he asked.

She shrugged. "No more than the next person. After all, I am a single woman. I like to have my fun."

Alex felt a shift in energy. He glanced at his friends and they too felt it. He decided to go on in the same vein with his questions.

"Is there a bar you go to around here?"

"There were two that were my favorites. Unfortunately, I had to stop going to the one down the street."

"Why?"

Rose's energy turned fidgety. She evaded eye contact with the group. "Look, I just can't go there anymore. Besides, this has nothing to do with what I'm going through. You're supposed to be helping me get rid of the demon."

There was a change in energy. Alex knew not to attach to Rose's fears and anxieties. By staying present, he was better able to discern what was energetically going on.

"You people better get rid of my demon!" Rose yelled out.

At that moment, Alex looked across the room and saw the apparition of a scruffy man in his early twenties. He was dressed in dirty jeans and a dark T-shirt. He was pointing at Rose and laughing.

"Yeah, that's right. I'm her demon and you better get rid of me." He broke out in even more laughter.

Zoey, Nell, and Ariel exchanged looks. They'd seen and heard him, too.

Alex knew he had to go deeper if he had any chance of helping the woman. "Rose," he began in a gentle, soothing voice, "is there something that happened in that bar that made you stop going?"

She thrust her chin out. "I don't like talking about it."

"It may be the only way to understand what's going on here."

Rose hesitated. It was obvious to all she didn't want to speak. But finally, the bravado disappeared and her shoulders slumped. "I met somebody there," she said in a defeated voice. "We used to get drunk together."

"—yeah, she used to buy me all the drinks I wanted," the spirit of the young man sneered.

"He was a lot younger than me. People started talking. It wasn't good, so I told him he had to leave me alone. But he wouldn't. I prayed and prayed, but he wouldn't stop. Finally, a friend told me she could get rid of him for me."

"What did she do?"

"I'm not sure. She told me if I gave her a hundred dollars, she'd protect me and have him go away. And he did."

"How did he die?" Alex asked softly.

"He OD'ed on heroin."

"My team and I need to confer about this. We're going to step outside, but we'll be right back."

Rose didn't offer any resistance. The group slowly made their way to the front yard.

"The kid obviously had some kind of relationship with her," Alex said. "I don't know what exactly went down between them, but she feels guilty that somehow she's responsible for his death, and she's angry about what's been going on in her home."

"Tell me about it," Nell said. "The energy in there is horrible. Her energy is horrible."

"And what about that friend?" Ariel asked. "How do you suppose she got rid of him?"

"It might be all coincidence, but Rose believes the friend got rid of him."

"There's something else," Zoey spoke up slowly. "I can't put my finger on what it is, but it's lurking in there, just beyond reach. I could feel it when we did our walkabout in her house. It was as if a long, dark shadow was following us around."

"What do we do?" Ariel asked.

"We've got to move whatever dark energy is in there first before we can concentrate on the kid. If you have to, keep your focus on me. Do not let any fears overcome you. Just keep your energy focused squarely on me."

Alex started to turn away. Nell reached out and grabbed his sleeve. "It is a demon in there, isn't it?"

Alex looked at her steadily but didn't answer.

They returned to the living room where they got into the circle, placing Rose in the middle.

"This isn't any of that dark arts stuff, is it?" the woman asked tremulously.

"No," Alex replied. "This is all about love."

They all took a moment to center themselves and raise their vibrations. Once again, as he settled into the higher energies, words appeared in Alex's mind, and he began to speak.

"That which is here that binds, we ask that you release. That which is here that deceives, we ask that you be illuminated. That which is here that demands payment, the payment is given in light. That which is here we now ask that you leave."

I can't leave. Something is holding me here.

Alex felt Nell shaking next to him. He tightened his grip on her hand. "Stay focused on me, Nell. Remember the light within your heart."

She nodded and he felt her trying to shift away from the darkness she was feeling. He energetically checked in on each of them, but to his dismay, no one, including himself, was able to get to a higher energetic space. Whatever was holding onto the spirit was also interfering with their ability to change their frequency. However, Alex noticed that the energy blocking them wasn't all over the place. It lacked the complexity of human emotion they'd become accustomed to dealing with from both the living and the dead. This was different. This energy was focused. Purposeful. It was keeping the spirit of the young man anchored by both the man's guilt and Rose's anger and guilt.

Alex tried once more to marshal his energies. He felt Zoey, Ariel, and Nell doing the same. Slowly, they pushed past the chokehold the dark entity had and finally raised their vibration to a point where they physically felt it slither away from the intense light they were shining on it. Once Alex was sure the dark entity was gone, he turned his attention to the spirit of the young man. "You are now forgiven. We ask that you see that your choices of what you believe to be your truth, is not your truth. That which bound you by your actions is no longer here to bind you. It has been released and moved on. We ask that you do the same. We ask that you let this woman go and move on."

But the ghost couldn't. His energy was changed; he was lighter, but he still couldn't move on. And there was nothing they could do to help him. They closed the circle and Alex turned to Rose.

"How do you feel?"

"It does feel better. But I'm still afraid."

"I can tell you what you were dealing with wasn't a demon. It was the boy you knew in the bar."

"Is—is he gone?"

"I'm afraid not. He won't be able to leave until you come to a place of forgiveness within yourself. You need to let go of what happened between the two of you. Your own guilt is binding him to you."

Rose stared at him in disbelief. Then, to the surprise of the group, she turned surly. "You're full of it. You don't know what you're talking about."

At that moment, the team knew this wasn't going to be resolved any time soon. On the way home, they discussed the situation.

"I feel bad for the kid," Ariel said. "I could feel he wanted to leave, but Rose's emotions won't let him."

"We learned something huge though," Alex replied.

"That we're not invincible," Zoey cut in.

They laughed. "We never claim to be," he continued. "Today helped us see that we can do our best to bring up our energy, but if the living refuse to let go of the things that bind the dead to them, there's absolutely nothing we can do. It seems it's easier to illuminate the dead and change their vibration than it is for the living. When they get into drama, they have their free will, which we can't interfere with. It's just another example on how the living hold onto the dead in their grief and guilt and anger." He noticed how quiet Nell was. She hadn't spoken a word since they'd gotten in the car. "Are you okay, Nell?"

She sighed. "I was thinking about how I felt during the circle. Even though I was shaking, it wasn't so much from cold. Rather, it was a dread that came over me. I felt like I was going dark inside. I know it doesn't make sense, but it was as though my entire inside was turning black." She looked across the car at Alex. "Was it a demon?"

He took his time answering. "I'm not sure, Nell. But whatever it was, it was very dark."

FORGIVENESS

We are so quick to jump to conclusions about who is hanging around. Ghosts are one of the most feared things in the world. No one understands what they are, how they are, and why they're here in the first place. Much of the misunderstandings about spirits unfortunately comes from religious teachings that tell us spirits are demonic and evil. Things that are misunderstood become the stuff of nightmares and superstitions. Having said that, demons do exist. We've run across a few in our own investigations. However, 99.9 percent of hauntings are what we call "common street ghosts." In other words, they are the spirits of human beings who feed off the drama of the living. Because what we are in life carries over into death, it's easy to see, for example, how the spirit of a murderer could be mistaken for a demon. Their energy of evil intent would carry over into death. Yet, do we continue to judge and feed them? Wouldn't it be better to offer some kind of forgiveness and begin to clear the space? Wouldn't it be helpful to break the chains that bind them to us? One of the most important, and difficult, things to do is to forgive. Yet knowing what the result would be—a lighter space, a lighter heart, a spirit no longer bound to you—isn't that worth finding a place of forgiveness? Would you rather be like Rose, tormented because you cannot let go of an emotion? Or would you rather be like thousands of other empaths who are learning to clear spaces of energy that does not belong there.

As we said earlier, we've had personal dealings with what we call the dark entities. Do we fully understand them yet? No. But we have come to understand their energy. Unlike the complexity of human emotions, demons are one dimensional in their energy. There is one focus in their energy. As long as we don't become the food they thrive on, we seem to be left alone. Empaths do tend to feel more darkness than regular people because of the choices people make in their lives. However, know this. As an empath, you are not a victim. You are a student in learning how to navigate the energies of everything around you that you see and cannot see. By learning to navigate those energies, you can then learn how to be of assistance.

THE CHAINS OF EXPERIENCE

Over the next few days, Alex continued to think about Rose and the unhappiness she was causing herself because of her inability to let go of guilt. He knew he and his team had done the best they could, but as Zoey said, they were not invincible. Nor did they ever claim to be. They were just a group of people learning to navigate the energies of both the seen and unseen worlds and offering assistance wherever they could.

Still, he felt a need to connect with nature. These lessons about the Other Side, though needed and appreciated, still left him a bit drained. He needed to get back to a place where he could recharge his batteries.

Over the following weekend, Alex drove to his favorite mountain and hiked up to the top. Finding a flat topped boulder, he sat down and stretched out his long legs. Below him, spread out in all directions, was a wide landscape of green. He breathed in the cool air and felt it move through his lungs. Slowly he felt the stresses of the last few days seep through him and out his feet. His head cleared and he beheld the beauty of the views before him.

He thought back to all the recent ghostly experiences he'd had and wondered why he didn't feel from ghosts what he felt right at that moment sitting on the mountain top.

Up here he felt unencumbered by life's worries. To tell the truth, even down there, off the mountain, he didn't feel those worries as much as others did. He'd come to a place in his life where he trusted. He knew there was a purpose to his life. Maybe it was figuring out what life was all about. Maybe it was teaching what he'd learned to others. Whatever it was, he'd been shown so many times that he was being taken care of by a power higher than himself. Sure, he wasn't rich. But he didn't need to be to be happy. He didn't own the latest jazzy car. But he didn't need that. His modest Jeep got him to wherever he needed to go. He wasn't dating the most beautiful woman in the world. He guffawed at that one. He'd dated enough beautiful women to know that was definitely something he didn't want. Too much pressure.

As for his friends, he knew he was blessed. They were truly friends in every sense of the word. They were there for him; they watched his back and accepted him for who he was. How many people could honestly say they had friends like that?

Which brought him back to the subject of ghosts. He considered the shadow people he and his group had seen throughout their lives. He realized that, as they continued to work to raise their vibrations, the shadow people were no longer shadows. They were now appearing to them as full apparitions. Was it possible that seeing a ghost as a shadow person had more to do with a living person's vibration? Did it have something to do with matching the frequencies of vibration so that a shadow person now appeared as a person and not a shadow?

His mind turned towards Mitch. He now understood why Mitch hadn't moved on. At first glance, it was because of his need to warn his sister about their brother. Yet, Alex felt there was something more. He remembered the deep sense of guilt Mitch was still holding onto, not only over the way he died, but by the way he'd lived his life. Senseless, is what Mitch had said.

If you looked at it one way, it was senseless. He made the choice to live a life of violence. He also made the fateful choice to drive his motorcycle while intoxicated. And he ended up paying for that decision with his life. But if you looked at it from another perspective, the deed was done. Mitch was dead. Why carry the guilt into the afterlife? Why not let it go and move on? Was the untruth of what Mitch was feeling keeping him stuck here? Was there something to the fact that the way we live our lives affects how we live our death?

He thought back to the ghost at the Grey Goose, stuck on the treadmill of seeking out the energy of alcohol he'd been addicted to in life. If he and his group, or someone else who understood energy hadn't come along to help, he'd be stuck on that treadmill for eternity, wandering, searching for that next ghostly drink.

As much as he didn't want to, his mind inevitably drifted back to Rose. He couldn't judge her. She was a woman filled with anger, most likely directed at herself for the decisions she'd taken throughout her life. He understood her inability to face what she thought she'd done. By paying for her friend to get rid of the young man, she believed that in some way, she'd caused his death.

If only she could understand that she didn't force him to take the heroin that killed him. That was his choice. By doing what she's doing, she's taking on not only the energy of all the choices she's made in her life, she's also taking on the choices the kid made for himself as well. It's no wonder he's bound to her.

Once again he marveled at how intertwined the energies of the living and dead were. Yet, as he'd learned up at Rose's, it was much easier to unravel the energies of what kept the dead bound to earth. The living, however, were so much more—

Alex's thoughts were interrupted when he heard the sounds of other hikers coming up the path below from where he sat. Peeking over the edge, he saw a father and son walking along. They were busy concentrating on where they were stepping, the silence punctuated by the sound of their boots scraping against the rocks. He was about to sit back and continue his thoughts when the silence was shattered by the sudden bellowing of the father.

"Why are you complaining?" he yelled to the cowering boy. "It was you who wanted to take this hike. Do you think I'm not tired and thirsty either? Do you think I'm not sweating my butt off? I hate hiking anyway. I don't know why you talked me into this. And now you have the nerve to complain?"

Alex shook his head to himself. Jeez, could the guy get any more negative? Even if they were both hot and tired and thirsty, couldn't they see this was an opportunity to just spend some quality time together? They were at the top anyway. All they had to do was sit down, drink some water from the water bottle hanging from their backpacks, and enjoy the scenery. Was that really so difficult? Was this guy simply one of those people who saw negativity in everything?

Suddenly, a little piece of the puzzle clicked into place.

Is that why spirits remain stuck? Is it like the first ghost who makes an appearance in Charles Dickens' *The Christmas Carol?* Remembering the countless movies Alex had seen over the years adapted from the famous book, the first ghost to appear to Ebenezer Scrooge was his old business partner, Jacob Marley. Seven years after his death, Marley came to Scrooge, showing him the large, heavy chains he'd forged in life that he was now condemned to carry in death. It was a scene that had always left Alex feeling a bit uneasy.

Thinking about the hiker, Alex wondered if the man's negativity was already forging chains that he would be condemned to carry in death if he didn't change his ways.

> Not only do we feel the negativity from the living, we, as empaths, feel negativity from the dead as well. Whatever their chains are made up of, whether it's from emotional baggage, or simply from being a jerk, we feel it.

Alex sat up as he had what he liked to call an "a-ha" moment.

> My God, all these experiences I've been having are really teaching me more about how to live my life. The choices we make in life carry through to the afterlife. If we die in traumatic situations, could it be we hold onto that trauma? If we die in a state of anger, guilt, or negativity, could we continue to hold onto those emotions in death as well? We say yes because we've seen that in our investigations. That's why there are stuck spirits. They never transcended those earthly emotions. They're still holding onto them, even though they're no longer part of the physical earthly realm.

Alex thought about those spirits they'd encountered that were stuck over what the paranormal community called "unfinished business."

> It doesn't matter if a spirit didn't get to finish something before they died. Their life is done. It's over. It doesn't matter anymore. All that matters is going on to a better place.

He looked out over the scenery, his mind filled with what he'd just figured out.

> Maybe that's part of what's happening in the world today. There is so much negativity. So much fear. Everyone is feeling that one way or another—empaths more than most. If we react to negativity and fear with more negativity and fear, it's just creating a huge swamp. When you add the negativity and fears from the dead, it's simply making a bad situation worse. Part of our responsibility as empaths is to not add any more drama to the drama that's already out there—not only from the living but from the dead as well. Because of our empathic abilities, we can change and move that energy, not hide from it.
>
> There's also a responsibility to how we live our lives. How we live will affect how we experience our death. It seems that if we're asses in life, we don't get a one-way ticket to Heaven when we die. Those heavy emotions

keep us stuck here. So maybe there really is something like a penance that needs to be paid—a way of making up for the way we lived our lives.

We also have a responsibility to live in such a way that we let go of all the things that really don't matter anymore so that when it's our turn to die, we don't become stuck ourselves.

Wow. There really is more to being an empath than I ever thought.

"But there's more."

There was a sudden shift in energy that was so high in vibration, his mind screeched to a halt. He immediately relaxed into the moment. Looking up, he saw the familiar man in the shimmering white robe standing before him. He waited for the spirit to speak. Instead, from behind him, the man took out what looked like a scroll. Smiling at Alex, he unfurled it.

"You've done well, my boy. You haven't shied away from your lessons. As you say, you keep on keeping on. I like that. However, there's another aspect to the chains we carry into death. It's called Empathic Contracts and you're going to be learning about those sooner than you think."

THE COMMON THREAD

We've been doing investigations for more than fifteen years. We've run into every kind of ghost you can imagine—sad ones, depressed ones, angry ones, violent ones, ones that hold onto unfinished business. However, there is a common thread that runs through all the hauntings we've investigated. There is a heavy earthly emotion they are still holding on to that doesn't allow them to move on. Because of that heavy earthly emotion, they don't even know they have a choice to move on.

We've experienced ghosts who were murdered and won't leave until their murderer is found. We've met ghosts who were so attached to their homes, they continue that ownership in death. The most poignant ghost we ever encountered was that of a World War I soldier who'd cursed his God over the atrocities he'd witnessed. When he was blown apart during a battle, his fear that God wouldn't forgive him kept him stuck.

What if we made an effort to release those emotions throughout our life? Forgive whoever we need to forgive? Tie up our loose ends. Take full responsibility for the choices we've made so that, when it comes our time to pass on, we don't become one of countless spirits, condemned to wander the earth in eternity.

EMPATHIC CONTRACTS

Alex waited. Instead of continuing his lecture, however, the energy changed again. Now Alex felt wind and cool air against his face. The spirit in the white robe had disappeared.

Now what the heck was that all about? There were times when Alex wondered if the man in the robe was actually a guide or a figment of his imagination. Yet the energy he felt whenever the man appeared told him it couldn't be made up in his head. Alex knew energy didn't lie; it was incapable of deceit. Whenever the robed man came to him, it was as though Alex was taken to another place. It was similar to his experiences during deep meditation or when he let go in any particular moment to experience the higher vibrations of energy. He would come out of it as though he were coming back to his place of reality after visiting, perhaps, another dimension or another realm of existence.

Whatever had just happened, Alex couldn't deny that his curiosity was piqued. What was this empathic contract the guide had mentioned? What did it mean for him?

As he started down the mountain towards his car, Alex thought back to other occasions when a guide had popped up, announcing he was about to learn something, then disappearing without telling him what the lesson was. He'd begun to suspect this was guidance's way of getting his attention, of giving him a road sign that told him to be prepared.

Well, he was certainly prepared. Whatever these empathic contracts were, he was eager to learn about them. He had a sense it was tied into what he was discovering lately about the afterlife. Could it be that the energy of these empathic contracts followed a person into death? What exactly did that mean?

That night, after eating a light supper, Alex sat on his couch, flipping through the channels, trying to find something to occupy his mind. He was just settling into an old rerun of the original *Star Trek* series when the image of his ex-wife, Carrie, abruptly popped into his head. He hadn't seen or spoken to her since their divorce years before. Why was she in his thoughts? What was going on?

Suddenly the phone rang. As Alex reached out to grab it, he was filled with an anxiety he couldn't quite understand. He took a deep breath and said, "Hello?"

"Hi Alex. It's Carrie."

As soon as he heard her voice, he felt his energy go into a tailspin. Before he could stop himself, he was flooded with memories of the hurt and pain she'd inflicted on him. The recollection of those troubled times sent him instantly into a feeling of victimhood. It had taken him a long time to recover from the wreckage of their marriage, and it surprised him that just the sound of her voice was able to dredge up all the old feelings of persecution and anguish.

"I haven't talked to you in long time," she continued in her soft, seductive voice.

Alex's spider sense went on full alert. He found himself apprehensively second guessing her words. Why was she calling after all this time? Was she going to try and insinuate herself back into his life? Was she going to attempt to wreck his life a second time? She only spoke in that tone of voice when she wanted something from him. It took all his efforts not to fall deeper through the rabbit hole of paranoia and suspicion.

"I hate to call under these circumstances, but I have some sad news to share, and I knew you'd want to know."

Alex's heart was racing in his chest as he unconsciously gripped the phone tighter in his hand.

"What's happened?" he managed to ask through the balled up emotions in his throat.

"Do you remember Sally Tracy?"

An image of a petite woman with auburn hair and a sweet smile danced in his mind's eye.

"Of course I remember Sally."

"She passed away last night from cancer. The wake and funeral are this week and I thought you should know in case you wanted to attend. I remember how close you two were, especially when you and I were going through our tough times." She unexpectedly chuckled. "It actually made me jealous."

Alex was touched that Carrie would think enough to let him know about Sally's passing, but he still held back, remembering how easy it had always been for her to switch any conversation back to herself.

"I'm sorry to hear that. We lost touch because her husband didn't approve of our friendship." He paused. "Will you be going to the funeral?"

"Yes, I'll be there."

Alex hesitated, then said, "I really appreciate your call. I know we didn't end on the best of terms."

"I know. I have a lot of regrets about that. You didn't deserve what I did to you. The only excuse I have is that I was young and stupid and didn't know any better."

They spoke a few more words before hanging up.

Alex sat back on his couch, musing over the conversation and, more importantly, the energy that encircled him. He realized he was still feeling the same emotions he'd felt during his marriage whenever Carrie didn't come home, or when she held herself aloof from him. He remembered all those times when his empathy told him she wasn't being truthful when he'd ask her where she'd been.

Yet their conversation just now was friendly and authentic. She'd even apologized for her behavior—something Alex never believed she would ever do.

What was going on?

Because he was still holding onto the past, it made him lack trust. It made his energy even more uncomfortable. That discomfort made him realize there was something here to learn.

He needed to talk to someone to help him flesh it out. He picked up the phone and was in the process of dialing Zoey when he suddenly felt the energy once more change around him. The hair on his arms and on the back of his neck stood up. Out of the corner of his eye, he saw a shadow dart by.

Fighting to get a grip on what he was feeling, he closed his eyes. He needed to let go of the conversation with Carrie, let go of all the emotions that phone call had evoked in order for him to raise his vibration. Taking a few deep breaths and beginning the process of grounding, he soon felt the heavier energies leave him. His body started to tingle as his vibration rose.

Feeling better, he opened his eyes.

And saw Sally standing in front of him.

She was pale, her wide eyes staring at him in bruised distress. In that moment, Alex was overcome with a feeling of such loss and regret, his own eyes filled with tears.

He had to get back to basics.

Just as he'd let go of the emotions surrounding the phone call with Carrie, he now pulled back from judging the energy he was feeling from Sally. He allowed it to move through him, grounding it out through his feet. As he did so, he noticed Sally's image growing brighter. Her energy blended into the light and the room filled with the most intense emotion of love he'd ever felt. Just as quickly as she'd appeared, she blinked out and was gone. But traces of the love and brightness remained.

He took a deep breath and expelled it slowly. He then dialed Zoey. When she answered, he recounted everything that had just happened.

"Jeez, Alex. Most people just eat leftover pizza and watch a baseball game at night. But you talk to ex-wives and get ghostly visitations," she teased. "I think it's because you watch too much *Star Trek*."

"Tell me about it. Saying it was a weird night doesn't even begin to explain what just occurred."

"Well, you are empathic. Do what you always do when you find yourself in a situation you don't quite understand. Break it all down to figure it out."

"I feel like something is about to change in me if I can figure out what just happened. There's more to it than Carrie calling and Sally showing up. But I'm racking my brains trying to comprehend what it could be."

"As you constantly tell me, it isn't in your brain. It's in your energy."

He expelled a breath. "You're right."

"You're always telling me that one of the biggest issues we as humans have is that when something happens, we go back to the card file in our minds and react the same way we did when the situation originally occurred. It's as if we've programmed ourselves to react a certain way. In your case, you were programmed to react with paranoia and anxiety because of everything you went through with Carrie. That was how you reacted originally when those things happened and just the sound of her voice triggered the same reaction."

Alex agreed. "Ah, so what I did was go back into my head and predetermine how I was going to feel because of the memories. It completely messed up my energy. Yet, you know, now that I think about it, Carrie was different. Her energy felt different. Only I was so caught up in my programming that I didn't notice until now."

"How was your energy when the spirit of Sally appeared?"

"I had a better handle on it because I let go of the judgments of the past. I was in a better place." Suddenly, Alex had an epiphany. "Whoa, I just realized something. I knew I had to let go of the energy I created talking to Carrie so I could help Sally. Just as we do when we stand in our circles during investigations. When I stopped judging and stayed in the moment, I actually felt the loss and regret Sally was feeling move through me. She lightened up."

"Why do you think she was feeling that loss and regret?" Zoey asked.

"When I was going through the breakup with Carrie, she was going through the same issues with her husband, Mark. It was as if our situations mirrored each other's. We became each other's support system."

"Did she divorce Mark?"

"No. She decided to stay in the marriage. I remember, she was into herbs and was building a nice little business for herself. But Mark was incredibly narcissistic. He hated the time she spent on her clients. It had to always be about him. He slowly and insidiously broke down her confidence until she basically became housebound. Now I understand the feelings of loss and regret I experienced when she appeared. Because of her choice to stay with him, and her choice in allowing him to break down her confidence, she never got to live her life." Alex had another small epiphany. "Wow, is that how I've been with Carrie? I've lived my life, but when she called, I realized there was still this cord that bound me to all the things she put me through."

Alex instantly felt the energy change within and around him. All the anxiety and paranoia evoked by Carrie left him in a way that was more complete than just grounding them out.

"Wow, I can feel your energy from here," Zoey exclaimed. "What just happened? What are you feeling now?"

Alex's voice was filled with wonder. "I'm feeling forgiveness."

"What do you mean?"

"All that past history with Carrie—all the worry and anxiety and my determination to avoid her or the need to change her is gone. So are the emotions I was feeling with Sally. I feel lighter."

"Isn't this interesting?" Zoey replied with a chuckle. "In all our investigations, we've been talking about forgiveness. But it was forgiveness in the abstract. Now here you are physically feeling your past. This is completely personal for you. You forgave and it healed your energy. It unbound you from the old energy of your past. You changed."

"I know."

"How did it happen?"

Before he could stop himself, he blurted out, "Contract."

"Contract? What does that mean?"

"It's been years since my divorce from Carrie, yet somewhere inside I was still holding on to all that angst. But in that moment, in that brief second, I got to a place where I changed the energy by just allowing it to be without judgment. I learned forgiveness. What forgiveness is at this moment is not anchoring to anything in my past. I let it all go. All the stuff that happened with her in the past isn't important anymore. When I did that, I got a gift. My energy changed and the burden of carrying all that baggage around is gone. Is it possible that life is set up contractually with certain people so you get to make different feeling choices? Each person in the contract plays their role—sort of like a teacher of feeling."

"I think you need to explain that to me a little more."

"Carrie was different. She wasn't the same person she was when we broke up. But by holding on to the past, I was making her the same. I reacted to her the same way I used to. I always thought she was the bad person, but in that moment, I was the victim because I was still holding on to everything. I was giving her that energy. She's in a different place, but I fell back to my old programming." As he said this, Alex felt his energy ratchet up again.

"I just felt your energy change again!" Zoey exclaimed.

"That's because I was wondering if it's possible Sally was part of my life because we also had a contract between us."

Alex thought back to those moments when people had wronged him. Each of those moments held a lesson for him to learn. Even the dead appearing to him were there to teach him. Was it possible that each of these people, both living and deceased, were part of a contract that was helping him to learn energy? That somehow, through an empathic contract, they served as teachers that allowed him to make different energetic choices? And, didn't it stand to reason that just as they gave him the opportunity to make different choices, he was fulfilling his part of the contract by being in their lives to allow them to do the same for themselves?

"I don't care about all the books I've read, all the classes I've been to, all the things I've seen. The only thing that changes me is my ability to react or change my reaction with people. It's like it's supposed to happen. Take Carrie for example. There is no reason under the sun that I should have become involved with that woman. We were totally wrong for each other, but it was as if I had to get married. I had to go through with it. Why? Because I learned so much from that experience, painful as it was, and it feels as though Carrie learned as well. Sally had the same opportunity to learn as I did. Maybe our friendship was part of the energetic contract that drew us to each other since we were going through the same thing. We were there to learn from each other. However, she chose to stay with Mark. She never progressed, never got to fully live her life. Maybe that depression that stemmed from the choice she made is what ultimately killed her. Yet when I settled back into my true power after speaking with Carrie, I changed. Something in me was redeemed. By taking on Sally's feelings of regret and loss, it helped heal her energy and she was finally able to move on."

"That's what happened with our investigations," Zoey reminded him. "We took on their emotions of regret and grief. By doing that, they were forgiven and were able to move on."

Alex whistled through the phone line. "There's so much more to this empathy stuff than even I realized. I think we need to get our little group together and discuss all of this. This has the potential to rock our world and I want Nell and Ariel to have the opportunity to learn as we just did."

ACCIDENT

We often wonder why, as empaths, we find the people who come into our lives aren't always the best for us. They are the ones who seem to hurt us, the ones we love so deeply who can't love us back. We keep attracting those same people to us over and over again. Why? Because there's a lesson to be learned. A contract was forged before you came to this life to have these experiences so you could learn a bigger lesson. Many times that lesson is about forgiveness. Forgiveness of them and forgiveness of ourselves.

In our ability to try and fix and change, the problem arises where we make it part of our responsibility to make everything better around us. We don't realize that true responsibility is in understanding how we work energetically. In our need to make things better, we forget that perhaps things need to be the way they are because they serve as better teachers to remind us how we use our energy in that moment. We learn to be a brighter light that allows us to transmute the energy around us. We learn that just as we have lessons to learn, so too do the people in our lives. We learn that we can't always pick up the pieces of others' life because we deny them the opportunity to learn what they need to learn. We are all given the same opportunities to learn, to make different choices. As we evolve into healed empaths, our own energy changes. It becomes brighter because it's no longer burdened with emotional baggage. We now have the ability to shine that light, not only on the living, but on the departed as well. We learn compassion; we understand more fully those lessons the dead didn't learn, those unfulfilled lessons that keep them stuck. Just as our choices change, through our higher energy, they now have the opportunity to see who they are and what they need to let go of so they can move on to that better place of peace and love.

WANDERING

"I've been thinking about all we've been through

"I've been thinking about all we've been through since we started this group," Nell responded a few days later. They'd all gathered at Alex's house and were seated in the living room. "I've had experiences that are beyond words. But I have to admit, I keep asking myself one question." She looked to each of her companions. "Why me? I mean, I'm overwhelmed by the thought that I'm actually helping spirits. I'm amazed I'm communicating with the Other Side. But when I look at everyone out there, going about their lives without a clue to how awesome this all is, I come back to wondering why is this happening to me? Why me?"

Alex looked at Nell. "Why not you?"

She had no response to that.

"We're here together because we all share a curiosity about figuring out our lives. Being empathic isn't so simple, is it? Yet at the same time, the experiences we've had haven't been so bad either. We've gotten through them all because we've understood these empathic energetic experiences are trying to teach us something. It's building up some kind of strength within us and preparing us for something. Whatever that something is, I'm sure we'll be ready to face it when the time comes.

Why us? Because we listen. Because we want to comprehend. There are millions out there like us, so I know we're not special.

"It's like taking up a mantle in a way. We've accepted the fact that we're empathic. We don't fight against it, we don't constantly throw up protection. There's a reason we feel what we feel. We've learned not to be afraid when empathic energetic experiences come up. We change our energy and we get through it. We don't plug in and add more drama to an already dramatic situation. It isn't easy—we all know it isn't. But by keeping an open heart and mind and not judging and allowing the experience to unfold, look at what we've been able to learn and feel and achieve."

"So basically," Zoey replied, "It's really keeping an eye on what we do with our energy on a daily basis."

"Exactly."

"That's not an easy thing to do," Zoey admitted.

"No, it isn't. We have to keep catching ourselves. But at least we're aware of it and know when we're leaking our energy and what we can do to shift our energy back to a better place." He turned to Ariel. "Didn't you tell me that just the other day you were able to ground out a headache you had?"

"Yes."

"Do you think you would have been able to do that if you hadn't gone through what you've been through?"

"I don't believe so."

"You didn't go into the drama of it. You didn't wail and cry out that you were going to die. You instead stayed in the moment, saw the headache for what it was—just energy—and you were able to move it. Which brings us back to the timeline. We were all meant to go through what we've been through in order to learn. Everyone has that opportunity. We chose to take it. And as we've seen, not only do our choices affect our daily lives, it affects our afterlife as well. Which brings me to why I asked you all here tonight.

"A few days ago, I had an experience that showed me there's more to ghost hunting than trying to prove or disprove the existence of ghosts. I also realized there's a lot more to empathy than I first imagined. All my belief systems have unraveled, yet the conclusion I came to is so simple. I wondered if we thought it had to be complicated when in actuality it's very simple." He saw the perplexed looks on their faces and smiled. "Before I explain, I asked you all here because I need to ask you each a question."

He looked first to Nell. "What do you think ghost hunting is all about?"

"It's something different, something new. It's fun."

"Was what you went through in Gettysburg fun? Did you enjoy what happened to you at Rose's?"

Nell thought about it for a moment, then shook her head. "You're right. Standing out on that battlefield, I lost who I was for a moment. I've never felt so much fear and anxiety and sadness in my life. I was completely overwhelmed. At Rose's, I felt my insides go dark. Yet, at the same time, I'd do it all again in a heartbeat because I got changed somehow. I got something out of it. I'm not sure what yet, but I'm not the same person I was before all that happened."

"You are changed. I believe your empathy allowed you to take on all that energy, and you had an experience. You felt the energy in that moment of what took place on that battlefield. You also felt what happens when someone is so mired in darkness, it attracts more darkness to them. Yet, when you got out of your drama and stopped judging it, you changed. And the energy around you changed. It felt better."

He turned to Ariel. "What are you getting out of this?"

"I'm curious. I want to know why I hear the names I hear. Is it real? Or is something else going on?"

"Have you learned anything from your experiences?"

"I think we're experiencing a lot more in life and in death from hearing and feeling and sensing things around us. The biggest lesson, however, is when we went to see Connie Collier. I immediately believed she was really communicating with spirits, yet now I realize she was just reading our energies. I need to be more careful not to jump to conclusions about what I'm experiencing."

"Exactly. That's something we all need to do. I did it with my ex-wife, and I really screwed up my energy when I did that. Obviously, many of these hauntings we're investigating are multi-layered. We can't go with the first thing we think it is, or what everyone around us thinks it is. Case in point is Mr. Astoria. There are these heinous stories about him that I frankly don't believe are true. Yet anyone who goes there and ignores what they feel could easily get caught up in that drama and miss what's really going on."

Ariel nodded. "I have more work to do, especially in the area of discerning what I'm feeling as far as energy goes."

"Zoey? How about you? Why do you do it?"

She grinned. "I do it because when you mess yourself up, someone has to pull you out of the mud." They laughed. Then Zoey turned serious. "I've spent my whole life thinking I'm seeing ghosts, afraid of seeing ghosts, wondering if I'm actually seeing ghosts. Well, guess what? Ever since we started this, now I know I am seeing ghosts. But bigger than that, I'm starting to realize we don't need to prove their existence or look for them. They've always been there. It's just up to me to settle into experiencing the Other Side. And as I settle into it, I'm discovering, like you Alex, that there's more to it. It's as if I'm learning what it means to be a ghost. And how to avoid being a ghost when it's my time to take the old dirt nap."

All three looked to Alex. "Why do you do it?" they asked simultaneously.

"I'm a glutton for punishment," he chuckled. "I like to feel things." He paused. "Throughout my entire life, I have found myself in situations in which I felt I had no choice but to experience. There was a contract on my timeline that said I had to have these experiences, be it with the living, with my fears, with relationships, etc. that was preparing me to experience the energy of the afterlife."

"And what conclusion have you reached?" Nell asked.

"There's a responsibility of life that follows you into death. In other words, each human being has a responsibility to the choices we make in life and the energy that comes out of those choices because that energy will carry into death. Think about the encounters we've had when we opened up our minds and our energy to the Other Side. Think about Mr. Astoria, Mitch, my friend Sally, the kid in Maine, or the alcoholic in Boston. Each one of them carried the angst, the worry, the anger, the grief, the sense of unfinished business with them into the afterlife. It's sad when you realize they never got past that point in their life. They died holding on to those emotions. Just like the living hold onto their emotional baggage, so do the dead. We as empaths feel all of that, no matter if they're living or dead. Yet, we each have a role to play. If we don't judge or get dramatic, and are able to let go of assumptions by staying in the moment, we stay open to whatever needs to be. We've all learned and physically felt that the higher vibration we experience when we stay open has the ability to change everything around us and everything we do. It even has the ability to help those on the Other Side to let go of their emotional baggage and move on. Just as I realized with my ex-wife that what happened in the past doesn't matter anymore, so too does our vibration help the dead realize that what happened in their life doesn't matter anymore either. As we take on their emotions, they lighten up and are then able to move on.

"Being empathic is the beginning of an opportunity to learn the barometer of energy that we experience or don't experience, according to our choices. It shows us cause and effect in thoughts, feelings, what we take into ourselves, how we treat our bodies, and how we treat each other. This carries into places as well. For the unevolved empath, they can get stuck on a treadmill of always looking for the perfect energy experience. However, they can't hide away from any experience. What happens is that they go into a state of victimhood because they feel so much. Yet, as the empath begins to understand that energy is here to teach, that we have choices in our life, that we don't need to be a victim to our life, that sense of victimhood goes away. That's one of the biggest gifts and opportunities an empath can evolve into.

"Learning about empathy and energy is not an ending. It's a beginning to understanding that there's more to life. It's more than just houses, or food, or the next toy. It's more than the next relationship, the next job, the next war we insist on fighting with each other. Our timeline shows there's an opportunity to learn. To choose to become something bigger before you die. That is the next chapter of all our lives."

"When do we begin that next chapter?" Zoey asked.

Alex felt the energy of his white-robed guide around him. He turned to his friends and smiled. "Sooner than you think."

AFTERWORD

So what does it mean to be an empathic ghost hunter?

It's certainly more than just proving or disproving the existence of ghosts.

Like energy attracts like energy. Drama attracts drama. Anger attracts anger. Love attracts love. Light attracts light. We believe there are many on this earth plane who are still looking for a higher vibration, a higher frequency that will allow them to navigate their lives, to make better choices to reach that space of happiness we all seek. We've learned that buying things is a fleeting experience of happiness. Is there an energy to this? We've learned that drawing people into our lives has ebbs and flows of happiness, love, sadness, and even anger. Is there an energy to this? Even for some reaching the pinnacle of success and still feeling unfulfilled? Is there an energy to this? Is it possible that the drama of ghost hunting and the need to prove they exist also carries an energy?

We say yes. Each of those experiences are but a fleeting example of a light that is already there within us waiting to shine when the right choice is made.

We'll be the first to admit that being an empath isn't easy. As you've seen throughout this book, and probably in your own life, you're feeling emotions not only from the living, but from the dead.

But as this book has demonstrated, there is so much more to being an empath than just feeling all the angst that's out in the world today. Not only can you change the energy around you by seeing what the moment is trying to teach you, you can also change the energy of the dead who are interacting with us much more than you can imagine.

One of the questions we're constantly asked is: Can a ghost force you to do something you wouldn't ordinarily do? We say, only if that desire is within you to begin with. If you love to drink, the energy of the ghost can make you believe you want to drink. If you're trying to diet or quit cigarettes, the energy of a ghost who craved those things in life could be experienced as your own cravings, making it difficult to stop.

In this way, is it possible that the dead are feeding off the energy of the living? A willful ghost can make your stomach feel tight because of the projection of their energetic need, carried over from life, to bully, to always be right or to diminish you with their overpowering personality. The ghost of someone who committed heinous acts in life can make your heart hurt because they have no idea of what love is. A ghost with unfinished business will make you feel sad because they never got a chance to complete whatever it was in life they believe they needed to do. As empaths, we react to what we feel from the dead because of the residue of the energy they're still holding onto. Is this something to shun? Or could it be a skill that allows us to piece together an energetic puzzle of what the energy is trying to teach you?

The living can shift gears pretty quickly if they don't feel they're getting what they need. Spirits don't do that as well. A part of them has to feed from the anchor that keeps them here, whether it is from addictions, grief, unfinished business, etc.

As an empathic ghost hunter, one of your most valuable tools will be to discern whether the energy you're feeling is from an actual ghost, or simply place memory, or reading someone else's auric field. The tool of discernment teaches you the truth of the how and why a spirit is stuck and, more importantly, the true meaning of life.

It teaches you the responsibilities of the choices you are still able to make in your own life. It teaches you to be aware of your own energetic reactions. Do you really want to add more negativity and fear to a world that is saturated by negativity and fear, not only from the living but from the dead as well? Do you want to add more gunk that you and other empaths will be forced to feel?

There are two things to keep in mind. The first is that part of your responsibility as a living human being is to make the choices that ensure that what you carry in life doesn't carry into death. If it does, you too may become a wandering spirit.

The second is to remember that the dead can no longer make those choices. The only choice left to them is, with the assistance of evolved empaths, to let go of whatever binds them here and move on. By learning to be the brightest light of love and non-judgment, you help clear the residue from a ghost and help them get to a better place.

What greater gift to give another soul than to help them get Home?

You can contact Bety and Steve on their website at www.comerfordwilson.com. You can also look them up on Facebook and Twitter. Alex has his own Facebook, Twitter, and Instagram page under Alex Empath. Check it out!

If you're interested in reading about some of our investigations, you can go to www.spiritlightnetwork.net.

BETY COMERFORD
AND STEVE WILSON

are ordained spiritualist ministers, shamanic healers, psychics, teachers, and paranormal investigators with more than thirty years experience helping those to understand their empathic gifts. With their many varied encounters with the paranormal, they assist those who experience ghosts and hauntings to comprehend the whys and hows of hauntings and paranormal experiences from an empathic point of view.

Author photograph by Josh Mantello